A TALE OF TWO CITIES

Charles Dickens

SPARK PUBLISHING

Spark Publishing
A Division of Barnes & Noble
120 Fifth Avenue
New York, NY 10011
www.sparknotes.com

ISBN-13: 978-1-4114-0313-0
ISBN-10: 1-4114-0313-4

Please submit changes or report errors to www.sparknotes.com/errors.

Printed in the United States.

10 9

Contents

CONTEXT

CHARLES DICKENS WAS BORN IN PORTSMOUTH, England in 1812. As the second of eight children in a very poor family, he lived a difficult childhood. Eventually, his father was sent to debtor's prison, and Dickens himself went to work at the age of twelve to help pay off the family's debt. This troublesome time scarred Dickens deeply and provided him with substantial material for such stories as *Great Expectations, Oliver Twist,* and *David Copperfield.* Steeped in social criticism, Dickens's writing provides a keen, sympathetic chronicle of the plight of the urban poor in nineteenth-century England. During his lifetime, Dickens enjoyed immense popularity, in part because of his vivid characterizations, and in part because he published his novels in installments, making them readily affordable to a greater number of people.

The Industrial Revolution, which swept through Europe in the late eighteenth century, originated in England. The rapid modernization of the English economy involved a shift from rural handicraft to large-scale factory labor. Technological innovations facilitated unprecedented heights of manufacture and trade, and England left behind its localized, cottage-industry economy to become a centralized, hyper-capitalist juggernaut of mass production. In tandem with this transformation came a significant shift in the nation's demographics. English cities swelled as a growing and impoverished working class flocked to them in search of work. As this influx of workers into urban centers continued, the bourgeoisie took advantage of the surplus of labor by keeping wages low. The poor thus remained poor, and often lived cramped in squalor. In many of his novels, Dickens chronicles his protagonists' attempts to fight their way out of such poverty and despair.

A Tale of Two Cities, originally published from April through November of 1859, appeared in a new magazine that Dickens had created called *All the Year Round.* Dickens started this venture after a falling-out with his regular publishers. Indeed, this period in Dickens's life saw many changes. While starring in a play by Wilkie Collins entitled *The Frozen Deep,* Dickens fell in love with a young actress named Ellen Ternan. Dickens's twenty-three-year marriage to Catherine Hogarth had become a source of unhappiness in recent years, and, by 1858, Hogarth had moved out of Dickens's home. The author arranged to keep Ternan in a separate residence.

Dickens's participation in Collins's play led not only to a shift in his personal life, but also to a career development, for it was this play that first inspired him to write *A Tale of Two Cities*. In the play, Dickens played the part of a man who sacrifices his own life so that his rival may have the woman they both love; the love triangle in the play became the basis for the complex relations between Charles Darnay, Lucie Manette, and Sydney Carton in *A Tale of Two Cities*. Moreover, Dickens appreciated the play for its treatment of redemption and rebirth, love and violence. He decided to transpose these themes onto the French Revolution, an event that embodied the same issues on a historical level. In order to make his novel historically accurate, Dickens turned to Thomas Carlyle's account of the revolution. Contemporaries had considered Carlyle's version to be the first and last word on the French peasants' fight for freedom.

Dickens had forayed into historical fiction only once before, with *Barnaby Rudge* (1841), and the project proved a difficult undertaking. The vast scope and somewhat grim aspects of his historical subject forced Dickens largely to abandon the outlandish and often comic characters that had come to define his writing. Although Jerry Cruncher and Miss Pross embody some typically Dickensian quirks—exaggerated mannerisms, idiosyncratic speech—they play only minor roles in the novel. While critics continue to debate the literary merits of the novel, no one denies the light that the novel sheds on Dickens's development as a novelist. More experimental than the novels that precede it, *A Tale of Two Cities* shows its author in transition. Dickens would emerge from this transition as a mature artist, ready to write *Great Expectations* (1860–1861) and *Our Mutual Friend* (1864–1865).

PLOT OVERVIEW

THE YEAR IS 1775, and social ills plague both France and England. Jerry Cruncher, an odd-job man who works for Tellson's Bank, stops the Dover mail-coach with an urgent message for Jarvis Lorry. The message instructs Lorry to wait at Dover for a young woman, and Lorry responds with the cryptic words, "Recalled to Life." At Dover, Lorry is met by Lucie Manette, a young orphan whose father, a once-eminent doctor whom she supposed dead, has been discovered in France. Lorry escorts Lucie to Paris, where they meet Defarge, a former servant of Doctor Manette, who has kept Manette safe in a garret. Driven mad by eighteen years in the Bastille, Manette spends all of his time making shoes, a hobby he learned while in prison. Lorry assures Lucie that her love and devotion can recall her father to life, and indeed they do.

The year is now 1780. Charles Darnay stands accused of treason against the English crown. A bombastic lawyer named Stryver pleads Darnay's case, but it is not until his drunk, good-for-nothing colleague, Sydney Carton, assists him that the court acquits Darnay. Carton clinches his argument by pointing out that he himself bears an uncanny resemblance to the defendant, which undermines the prosecution's case for unmistakably identifying Darnay as the spy the authorities spotted. Lucie and Doctor Manette watched the court proceedings, and that night, Carton escorts Darnay to a tavern and asks how it feels to receive the sympathy of a woman like Lucie. Carton despises and resents Darnay because he reminds him of all that he himself has given up and might have been.

In France, the cruel Marquis Evrémonde runs down a plebian child with his carriage. Manifesting an attitude typical of the aristocracy in regard to the poor at that time, the Marquis shows no regret, but instead curses the peasantry and hurries home to his chateau, where he awaits the arrival of his nephew, Darnay, from England. Arriving later that night, Darnay curses his uncle and the French aristocracy for its abominable treatment of the people. He renounces his identity as an Evrémonde and announces his intention to return to England. That night, the Marquis is murdered; the murderer has left a note signed with the nickname adopted by French revolutionaries: "Jacques."

PLOT OVERVIEW

A year passes, and Darnay asks Manette for permission to marry Lucie. He says that, if Lucie accepts, he will reveal his true identity to Manette. Carton, meanwhile, also pledges his love to Lucie, admitting that, though his life is worthless, she has helped him dream of a better, more valuable existence. On the streets of London, Jerry Cruncher gets swept up in the funeral procession for a spy named Roger Cly. Later that night, he demonstrates his talents as a "Resurrection-Man," sneaking into the cemetery to steal and sell Cly's body. In Paris, meanwhile, another English spy known as John Barsad drops into Defarge's wine shop. Barsad hopes to turn up evidence concerning the mounting revolution, which is still in its covert stages. Madame Defarge sits in the shop knitting a secret registry of those whom the revolution seeks to execute. Back in London, Darnay, on the morning of his wedding, keeps his promise to Manette; he reveals his true identity and, that night, Manette relapses into his old prison habit of making shoes. After nine days, Manette regains his presence of mind, and soon joins the newlyweds on their honeymoon. Upon Darnay's return, Carton pays him a visit and asks for his friendship. Darnay assures Carton that he is always welcome in their home.

The year is now 1789. The peasants in Paris storm the Bastille and the French Revolution begins. The revolutionaries murder aristocrats in the streets, and Gabelle, a man charged with the maintenance of the Evrémonde estate, is imprisoned. Three years later, he writes to Darnay, asking to be rescued. Despite the threat of great danger to his person, Darnay departs immediately for France.

As soon as Darnay arrives in Paris, the French revolutionaries arrest him as an emigrant. Lucie and Manette make their way to Paris in hopes of saving him. Darnay remains in prison for a year and three months before receiving a trial. In order to help free him, Manette uses his considerable influence with the revolutionaries, who sympathize with him for having served time in the Bastille. Darnay receives an acquittal, but that same night he is arrested again. The charges, this time, come from Defarge and his vengeful wife. Carton arrives in Paris with a plan to rescue Darnay and obtains the help of John Barsad, who turns out to be Solomon Pross, the long-lost brother of Miss Pross, Lucie's loyal servant.

At Darnay's trial, Defarge produces a letter that he discovered in Manette's old jail cell in the Bastille. The letter explains the cause of Manette's imprisonment. Years ago, the brothers Evrémonde (Darnay's father and uncle) enlisted Manette's medical assistance.

They asked him to tend to a woman, whom one of the brothers had raped, and her brother, whom the same brother had stabbed fatally. Fearing that Manette might report their misdeeds, the Evrémondes had him arrested. Upon hearing this story, the jury condemns Darnay for the crimes of his ancestors and sentences him to die within twenty-four hours. That night, at the Defarge's wine shop, Carton overhears Madame Defarge plotting to have Lucie and her daughter (also Darnay's daughter) executed as well; Madame Defarge, it turns out, is the surviving sibling of the man and woman killed by the Evrémondes. Carton arranges for the Manettes' immediate departure from France. He then visits Darnay in prison, tricks him into changing clothes with him, and, after dictating a letter of explanation, drugs his friend unconscious. Barsad carries Darnay, now disguised as Carton, to an awaiting coach, while Carton, disguised as Darnay, awaits execution. As Darnay, Lucie, their child, and Dr. Manette speed away from Paris, Madame Defarge arrives at Lucie's apartment, hoping to arrest her. There she finds the supremely protective Miss Pross. A scuffle ensues, and Madame Defarge dies by the bullet of her own gun. Sydney Carton meets his death at the guillotine, and the narrator confidently asserts that Carton dies with the knowledge that he has finally imbued his life with meaning.

CHARACTER LIST

Charles Darnay A French aristocrat by birth, Darnay chooses to live in England because he cannot bear to be associated with the cruel injustices of the French social system. Darnay displays great virtue in his rejection of the snobbish and cruel values of his uncle, the Marquis Evrémonde. He exhibits an admirable honesty in his decision to reveal to Doctor Manette his true identity as a member of the infamous Evrémonde family. So, too, does he prove his courage in his decision to return to Paris at great personal risk to save the imprisoned Gabelle.

Sydney Carton An insolent, indifferent, and alcoholic attorney who works with Stryver. Carton has no real prospects in life and doesn't seem to be in pursuit of any. He does, however, love Lucie, and his feelings for her eventually transform him into a man of profound merit. At first the polar opposite of Darnay, in the end Carton morally surpasses the man to whom he bears a striking physical resemblance.

Doctor Manette Lucie's father and a brilliant physician, Doctor Manette spent eighteen years as a prisoner in the Bastille. At the start of the novel, Manette does nothing but make shoes, a hobby that he adopted to distract himself from the tortures of prison. As he overcomes his past as a prisoner, however, he proves to be a kind, loving father who prizes his daughter's happiness above all things.

Lucie Manette A young French woman who grew up in England, Lucie was raised as a ward of Tellson's Bank because her parents were assumed dead. Dickens depicts Lucie as an archetype of compassion. Her love has the power to bind her family together—the text often refers to her as the "golden thread." Furthermore, her love has the power to transform those around her. It enables

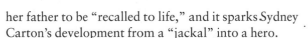

her father to be "recalled to life," and it sparks Sydney
Carton's development from a "jackal" into a hero.

Monsieur Defarge A wine-shop owner and revolutionary in
the poor Saint Antoine section of Paris, Monsieur
Defarge formerly worked as a servant for Doctor
Manette. Defarge proves an intelligent and committed
revolutionary, a natural leader. Although he remains
dedicated to bringing about a better society at any
cost, he does demonstrate a kindness toward Manette.
His wife, Madame Defarge, views this consideration
for Manette as a weakness.

Madame Defarge A cruel revolutionary whose hatred of the
aristocracy fuels her tireless crusade, Madame Defarge
spends a good deal of the novel knitting a register of
everyone who must die for the revolutionary cause.
Unlike her husband, she proves unrelentingly bloodthirsty, and her lust for vengeance knows no bounds.

Jarvis Lorry An elderly businessman who works for Tellson's
Bank, Mr. Lorry is a very business-oriented bachelor
with a strong moral sense and a good, honest heart.
He proves trustworthy and loyal, and Doctor Manette
and Lucie come to value him as a personal friend.

Jerry Cruncher An odd-job man for Tellson's Bank, Cruncher is
gruff, short-tempered, superstitious, and uneducated.
He supplements his income by working as a
"Resurrection-Man," one who digs up dead bodies
and sells them to scientists.

Miss Pross The servant who raised Lucie, Miss Pross is brusque,
tough, and fiercely loyal to her mistress. Because she
personifies order and loyalty, she provides the perfect
foil to Madame Defarge, who epitomizes the violent
chaos of the revolution.

Marquis Evrémonde Charles Darnay's uncle, the Marquis
Evrémonde is a French aristocrat who embodies an
inhumanly cruel caste system. He shows absolutely no

regard for human life and wishes that the peasants of the world would be exterminated.

Mr. Stryver An ambitious lawyer, Stryver dreams of climbing the social ladder. Unlike his associate, Sydney Carton, Stryver is bombastic, proud, and foolish.

John Barsad Like Roger Cly, John Barsad is a British spy who swears that patriotism is his only motive. Barsad falsely claims to be a virtuous man of upstanding reputation.

Roger Cly Like John Barsad, Roger Cly is a British spy who swears that patriotism alone inspires all of his actions. Cly feigns honesty but in fact constantly participates in conniving schemes.

Gabelle The man charged with keeping up the Evrémonde estate after the Marquis's death, Gabelle is imprisoned by the revolutionaries. News of his internment prompts Darnay to travel to France to save him.

ANALYSIS OF MAJOR CHARACTERS

SYDNEY CARTON

Sydney Carton proves the most dynamic character in *A Tale of Two Cities*. He first appears as a lazy, alcoholic attorney who cannot muster even the smallest amount of interest in his own life. He describes his existence as a supreme waste of life and takes every opportunity to declare that he cares for nothing and no one. But the reader senses, even in the initial chapters of the novel, that Carton in fact feels something that he perhaps cannot articulate. In his conversation with the recently acquitted Charles Darnay, Carton's comments about Lucie Manette, while bitter and sardonic, betray his interest in, and budding feelings for, the gentle girl. Eventually, Carton reaches a point where he can admit his feelings to Lucie herself. Before Lucie weds Darnay, Carton professes his love to her, though he still persists in seeing himself as essentially worthless. This scene marks a vital transition for Carton and lays the foundation for the supreme sacrifice that he makes at the novel's end.

Carton's death has provided much material for scholars and critics of Dickens's novel. Some readers consider it the inevitable conclusion to a work obsessed with the themes of redemption and resurrection. According to this interpretation, Carton becomes a Christ-like figure, a selfless martyr whose death enables the happiness of his beloved and ensures his own immortality. Other readers, however, question the ultimate significance of Carton's final act. They argue that since Carton initially places little value on his existence, the sacrifice of his life proves relatively easy. However, Dickens's frequent use in his text of other resurrection imagery—his motifs of wine and blood, for example—suggests that he did intend for Carton's death to be redemptive, whether or not it ultimately appears so to the reader. As Carton goes to the guillotine, the narrator tells us that he envisions a beautiful, idyllic Paris "rising from the abyss" and sees "the evil of this time and of the previous time of which this is the natural birth, gradually making expiation for itself and wearing out." Just as the apocalyptic violence of the revolution precedes a new society's birth, perhaps it is only in the sacrifice of his life that Carton can establish his life's great worth.

MADAME DEFARGE

Possessing a remorseless bloodlust, Madame Defarge embodies the chaos of the French Revolution. The initial chapters of the novel find her sitting quietly and knitting in the wine shop. However, her apparent passivity belies her relentless thirst for vengeance. With her stitches, she secretly knits a register of the names of the revolution's intended victims. As the revolution breaks into full force, Madame Defarge reveals her true viciousness. She turns on Lucie in particular, and, as violence sweeps Paris, she invades Lucie's physical and psychological space. She effects this invasion first by committing the faces of Lucie and her family to memory, in order to add them to her mental "register" of those slated to die in the revolution. Later, she bursts into the young woman's apartment in an attempt to catch Lucie mourning Darnay's imminent execution.

Dickens notes that Madame Defarge's hatefulness does not reflect any inherent flaw, but rather results from the oppression and personal tragedy that she has suffered at the hands of the aristocracy, specifically the Evrémondes, to whom Darnay is related by blood, and Lucie by marriage. However, the author refrains from justifying Madame Defarge's policy of retributive justice. For just as the aristocracy's oppression has made an oppressor of Madame Defarge herself, so will her oppression, in turn, make oppressors of her victims. Madame Defarge's death by a bullet from her own gun—she dies in a scuffle with Miss Pross—symbolizes Dickens's belief that the sort of vengeful attitude embodied by Madame Defarge ultimately proves a self-damning one.

DOCTOR MANETTE

Dickens uses Doctor Manette to illustrate one of the dominant motifs of the novel: the essential mystery that surrounds every human being. As Jarvis Lorry makes his way toward France to recover Manette, the narrator reflects that "every human creature is constituted to be that profound secret and mystery to every other." For much of the novel, the cause of Manette's incarceration remains a mystery both to the other characters and to the reader.

Even when the story concerning the evil Marquis Evrémonde comes to light, the conditions of Manette's imprisonment remain hidden. Though the reader never learns exactly how Manette suffered, his relapses into trembling sessions of shoemaking evidence the depth of his misery.

Like Carton, Manette undergoes a drastic change over the course of the novel. He is transformed from an insensate prisoner who mindlessly cobbles shoes into a man of distinction. The contemporary reader tends to understand human individuals not as fixed entities but rather as impressionable and reactive beings, affected and influenced by their surroundings and by the people with whom they interact. In Dickens's age, however, this notion was rather revolutionary. Manette's transformation testifies to the tremendous impact of relationships and experience on life. The strength that he displays while dedicating himself to rescuing Darnay seems to confirm the lesson that Carton learns by the end of the novel—that not only does one's treatment of others play an important role in others' personal development, but also that the very worth of one's life is determined by its impact on the lives of others.

CHARLES DARNAY AND LUCIE MANETTE

Novelist E. M. Forster famously criticized Dickens's characters as "flat," lamenting that they seem to lack the depth and complexity that make literary characters realistic and believable. Charles Darnay and Lucie Manette certainly fit this description. A man of honor, respect, and courage, Darnay conforms to the archetype of the hero but never exhibits the kind of inner struggle that Carton and Doctor Manette undergo. His opposition to the Marquis' snobbish and cruel aristocratic values is admirable, but, ultimately, his virtue proves too uniform, and he fails to exert any compelling force on the imagination.

Along similar lines, Lucie likely seems to modern readers as uninteresting and two-dimensional as Darnay. In every detail of her being, she embodies compassion, love, and virtue; the indelible image of her cradling her father's head delicately on her breast encapsulates her role as the "golden thread" that holds her family together. She manifests her purity of devotion to Darnay in her unquestioning willingness to wait at a street corner for two hours each day, on the off chance that he will catch sight of her from his prison window. In a letter to Dickens, a contemporary criticized such simplistic characterizations:

> *The tenacity of your imagination, the vehemence and fixity with which you impress your thought into the detail you wish to grasp, limit your knowledge, arrest you in a single feature, prevent you from reaching all the parts of the soul, and from sounding its depths.*

While Darnay and Lucie may not act as windows into the gritty essence of humanity, in combination with other characters they contribute to a more detailed picture of human nature. First, they provide the light that counters the vengeful Madame Defarge's darkness, revealing the moral aspects of the human soul so noticeably absent from Madame Defarge. Second, throughout the novel they manifest a virtuousness that Carton strives to attain and that inspires his very real and believable struggles to become a better person.

THEMES, MOTIFS & SYMBOLS

THEMES

Themes are the fundamental and often universal ideas explored in a literary work.

THE EVER-PRESENT POSSIBILITY OF RESURRECTION

With *A Tale of Two Cities,* Dickens asserts his belief in the possibility of resurrection and transformation, both on a personal level and on a societal level. The narrative suggests that Sydney Carton's death secures a new, peaceful life for Lucie Manette, Charles Darnay, and even Carton himself. By delivering himself to the guillotine, Carton ascends to the plane of heroism, becoming a Christ-like figure whose death serves to save the lives of others. His own life thus gains meaning and value. Moreover, the final pages of the novel suggest that, like Christ, Carton will be resurrected—Carton is reborn in the hearts of those he has died to save. Similarly, the text implies that the death of the old regime in France prepares the way for the beautiful and renewed Paris that Carton supposedly envisions from the guillotine. Although Carton spends most of the novel in a life of indolence and apathy, the supreme selflessness of his final act speaks to a human capacity for change. Although the novel dedicates much time to describing the atrocities committed both by the aristocracy and by the outraged peasants, it ultimately expresses the belief that this violence will give way to a new and better society.

Dickens elaborates his theme with the character of Doctor Manette. Early on in the novel, Lorry holds an imaginary conversation with him in which he says that Manette has been "recalled to life." As this statement implies, the doctor's eighteen-year imprisonment has constituted a death of sorts. Lucie's love enables Manette's spiritual renewal, and her maternal cradling of him on her breast reinforces this notion of rebirth.

THE NECESSITY OF SACRIFICE

Connected to the theme of the possibility of resurrection is the notion that sacrifice is necessary to achieve happiness. Dickens examines this second theme, again, on both a national and personal level. For example, the revolutionaries prove that a new, egalitarian French republic can come about only with a heavy and terrible cost—personal loves and loyalties must be sacrificed for the good of the nation. Also, when Darnay is arrested for the second time, in Book the Third, Chapter 7, the guard who seizes him reminds Manette of the primacy of state interests over personal loyalties. Moreover, Madame Defarge gives her husband a similar lesson when she chastises him for his devotion to Manette—an emotion that, in her opinion, only clouds his obligation to the revolutionary cause. Most important, Carton's transformation into a man of moral worth depends upon his sacrificing of his former self. In choosing to die for his friends, Carton not only enables their happiness but also ensures his spiritual rebirth.

THE TENDENCY TOWARD VIOLENCE AND OPPRESSION IN REVOLUTIONARIES

Throughout the novel, Dickens approaches his historical subject with some ambivalence. While he supports the revolutionary cause, he often points to the evil of the revolutionaries themselves. Dickens deeply sympathizes with the plight of the French peasantry and emphasizes their need for liberation. The several chapters that deal with the Marquis Evrémonde successfully paint a picture of a vicious aristocracy that shamelessly exploits and oppresses the nation's poor. Although Dickens condemns this oppression, however, he also condemns the peasants' strategies in overcoming it. For in fighting cruelty with cruelty, the peasants effect no true revolution; rather, they only perpetuate the violence that they themselves have suffered. Dickens makes his stance clear in his suspicious and cautionary depictions of the mobs. The scenes in which the people sharpen their weapons at the grindstone and dance the grisly Carmagnole come across as deeply macabre. Dickens's most concise and relevant view of revolution comes in the final chapter, in which he notes the slippery slope down from the oppressed to the oppressor: "Sow the same seed of rapacious license and oppression over again, and it will surely yield the same fruit according to its kind." Though Dickens sees the French Revolution as a great symbol of transformation and resurrection, he emphasizes that its violent means were ultimately antithetical to its end.

MOTIFS

Motifs are recurring structures, contrasts, and literary devices that can help to develop and inform the text's major themes.

DOUBLES

The novel's opening words ("It was the best of times, it was the worst of times. . . .") immediately establish the centrality of doubles to the narrative. The story's action divides itself between two locales, the two cities of the title. Dickens positions various characters as doubles as well, thus heightening the various themes within the novel. The two most important females in the text function as diametrically opposed doubles: Lucie is as loving and nurturing as Madame Defarge is hateful and bloodthirsty. Dickens then uses this opposition to make judgments and thematic assertions. Thus, for example, while Lucie's love initiates her father's spiritual transformation and renewal, proving the possibility of resurrection, Madame Defarge's vengefulness only propagates an infinite cycle of oppression, showing violence to be self-perpetuating.

Dickens's doubling technique functions not only to draw oppositions, but to reveal hidden parallels. Carton, for example, initially seems a foil to Darnay; Darnay as a figure reminds him of what he could have been but has failed to become. By the end of the novel, however, Carton transforms himself from a good-for-nothing to a hero whose goodness equals or even surpasses that of the honorable Darnay. While the two men's physical resemblance initially serves only to underscore Carton's moral inferiority to Darnay, it ultimately enables Carton's supremely self-elevating deed, allowing him to disguise himself as the condemned Darnay and die in his place. As Carton goes to the guillotine in his double's stead, he raises himself up to, or above, Darnay's virtuous status.

SHADOWS AND DARKNESS

Shadows dominate the novel, creating a mood of thick obscurity and grave foreboding. An aura of gloom and apprehension surrounds the first images of the actual story—the mail coach's journey in the dark and Jerry Cruncher's emergence from the mist. The introduction of Lucie Manette to Jarvis Lorry furthers this motif, as Lucie stands in a room so darkened and awash with shadows that the candlelight seems buried in the dark panels of the walls. This atmosphere contributes to the mystery surrounding Lorry's mission to Paris and Manette's imprisonment. It also manifests Dickens's observations about the shadowy depths of the human heart. As illustrated in the chapter with the appropriate subheading "The Night Shadows," every living person carries profound secrets and mysteries that will never see the light of day. Shadows continue to fall across the entire novel. The vengeful Madame Defarge casts a shadow on Lucie and all of her hopes, as emphasized in Book the Third, Chapter 5. As Lucie stands in the pure, fresh snow, Madame Defarge passes by "like a shadow over the white road." In addition, the letter that Defarge uses to condemn Darnay to death throws a crippling shadow over the entire family; fittingly, the chapter that reveals the letter's contents bears the subheading "The Substance of the Shadow."

IMPRISONMENT

Almost all of the characters in *A Tale of Two Cities* fight against some form of imprisonment. For Darnay and Manette, this struggle is quite literal. Both serve significant sentences in French jails. Still, as the novel demonstrates, the memories of what one has experienced prove no less confining than the walls of prison. Manette, for example, finds himself trapped, at times, by the recollection of life in the Bastille and can do nothing but revert, trembling, to his pathetic shoemaking compulsion. Similarly, Carton spends much of the novel struggling against the confines of his own personality, dissatisfied with a life that he regards as worthless.

SYMBOLS

> *Symbols are objects, characters, figures, and colors used to represent abstract ideas or concepts.*

THE BROKEN WINE CASK

With his depiction of a broken wine cask outside Defarge's wine shop, and with his portrayal of the passing peasants' scrambles to lap up the spilling wine, Dickens creates a symbol for the desperate quality of the people's hunger. This hunger is both the literal hunger for food—the French peasants were starving in their poverty—and the metaphorical hunger for political freedoms. On the surface, the scene shows the peasants in their desperation to satiate the first of these hungers. But it also evokes the violent measures that the peasants take in striving to satisfy their more metaphorical cravings. For instance, the narrative directly associates the wine with blood, noting that some of the peasants have acquired "a tigerish smear about the mouth" and portraying a drunken figure scrawling the word "blood" on the wall with a wine-dipped finger. Indeed, the blood of aristocrats later spills at the hands of a mob in these same streets.

Throughout the novel, Dickens sharply criticizes this mob mentality, which he condemns for perpetrating the very cruelty and oppression from which the revolutionaries hope to free themselves. The scene surrounding the wine cask is the novel's first tableau of the mob in action. The mindless frenzy with which these peasants scoop up the fallen liquid prefigures the scene at the grindstone, where the revolutionaries sharpen their weapons (Book the Third, Chapter 2), as well as the dancing of the macabre Carmagnole (Book the Third, Chapter 5).

MADAME DEFARGE'S KNITTING

Even on a literal level, Madame Defarge's knitting constitutes a whole network of symbols. Into her needlework she stitches a registry, or list of names, of all those condemned to die in the name of a new republic. But on a metaphoric level, the knitting constitutes a symbol in itself, representing the stealthy, cold-blooded vengefulness of the revolutionaries. As Madame Defarge sits quietly knitting, she appears harmless and quaint. In fact, however, she sentences her victims to death. Similarly, the French peasants may appear simple and humble figures, but they eventually rise up to massacre their oppressors.

Dickens's knitting imagery also emphasizes an association between vengefulness and fate, which, in Greek mythology, is traditionally linked to knitting or weaving. The Fates, three sisters who control human life, busy themselves with the tasks of weavers or seamstresses: one sister spins the web of life, another measures it, and the last cuts it. Madame Defarge's knitting thus becomes a symbol of her victims' fate—death at the hands of a wrathful peasantry.

THE MARQUIS

The Marquis Evrémonde is less a believable character than an archetype of an evil and corrupt social order. He is completely indifferent to the lives of the peasants whom he exploits, as evidenced by his lack of sympathy for the father of the child whom his carriage tramples to death. As such, the Marquis stands as a symbol of the ruthless aristocratic cruelty that the French Revolution seeks to overcome.

Summary & Analysis

Preface

In a brief note, Dickens mentions the source of inspiration for *A Tale of Two Cities*: a play in which he acted, called *The Frozen Deep,* written by his friend Wilkie Collins. He adds that he hopes that he can further his readers' understanding of the French Revolution—"that terrible time"—but that no one can truly hope to surpass Thomas Carlyle's *The French Revolution* (published in 1837).

Book the First: Recalled to Life
Chapters 1–4

Summary: Chapter 1: The Period

> *It was the best of times, it was the worst of times, it was the age of wisdom, it was the age of foolishness....*
> *(See* QUOTATIONS, *p. 59)*

As its title promises, this brief chapter establishes the era in which the novel takes place: England and France in 1775. The age is marked by competing and contradictory attitudes—"It was the best of times, it was the worst of times"—but resembles the "present period" in which Dickens writes. In England, the public worries over religious prophecies, popular paranormal phenomena in the form of "the Cock-lane ghost," and the messages that a colony of British subjects in America has sent to King George III. France, on the other hand, witnesses excessive spending and extreme violence, a trend that anticipates the erection of the guillotine. Yet in terms of peace and order, English society cannot "justify much national boasting" either—crime and capital punishment abound.

Summary: Chapter 2: The Mail

On a Friday night in late November of 1775, a mail coach wends its way from London to Dover. The journey proves so treacherous that the three passengers must dismount from the carriage and hike alongside it as it climbs a steep hill. From out of the great mists, a messenger on horseback appears and asks to speak to Jarvis Lorry of Tellson's Bank. The travelers react warily, fearing that they have come upon a highwayman or robber. Mr. Lorry, however, recognizes the messenger's voice as that of Jerry Cruncher, the odd-job man at Tellson's, and accepts his message. The note that Jerry passes him reads: "Wait at Dover for Mam'selle." Lorry instructs Jerry to return to Tellson's with this reply: "Recalled to Life." Confused and troubled by the "blazing strange message," Jerry rides on to deliver it.

SUMMARY: CHAPTER 3: THE NIGHT SHADOWS

> A *wonderful fact to reflect upon, that every human creature is constituted to be that profound secret and mystery to every other....*
>
> *(See* QUOTATIONS*, p. 60)*

The narrator ponders the secrets and mysteries that each human being poses to every other: Lorry, as he rides on in the mail coach with two strangers, constitutes a case in point. Dozing, he drifts in and out of dreams, most of which revolve around the workings of Tellson's bank. Still, there exists "another current of impression that never cease[s] to run" through Lorry's mind—the notion that he makes his way to dig someone out of a grave. He imagines repetitive conversations with a specter, who tells Lorry that his body has lain buried nearly eighteen years. Lorry informs his imaginary companion that he now has been "recalled to life" and asks him if he cares to live. He also asks, cryptically, "Shall I show her to you? Will you come and see her?" The ghost's reaction to this question varies, as he sometimes claims that he would die were he to see this woman too soon; at other times, he weeps and pleads to see her immediately.

SUMMARY: CHAPTER 4: THE PREPARATION

The next morning, Lorry descends from the coach at the Royal George Hotel in Dover. After shedding his travel clothes, he emerges as a well-dressed businessman of sixty. That afternoon, a waiter announces that Lucie Manette has arrived from London. Lorry meets the "short, slight, pretty figure" who has received word from the bank that "some intelligence—or discovery" has been made "respecting the small property of my poor father . . . so long dead." After reiterating his duties as a businessman, Lorry relates the real reason that Tellson's has summoned Lucie to Paris. Her father, once a reputed doctor, has been found alive. "Your father," Lorry reports to her, "has been taken to the house of an old servant in Paris, and we are going there: I, to identify him if I can: you, to restore him to life, love, duty, rest, comfort." Lucie goes into shock, and her lively and protective servant, Miss Pross, rushes in to attend to her.

ANALYSIS: CHAPTERS 1–4

The opening sentence of the novel makes clear, as the title itself does, the importance of doubles in the text:

> *It was the best of times, it was the worst of times, it*
> *was the age of wisdom, it was the age of foolishness, it*
> *was the epoch of belief, it was the epoch of incredulity,*
> *it was the season of Light, it was the season of*
> *Darkness, it was the spring of hope, it was the winter*
> *of despair. . . .*

Doubles prove essential to the novel's structure, plot, and dominant themes. The idea of resurrection, a theme that emerges in these early pages, would not be possible without some form of its opposite—death. In order to pave the way for the first such resurrection—the recalling to life of the long-imprisoned Doctor Manette—Dickens does much to establish a dark, ominous tone suggestive of death. From the mist-obscured route of the Dover mail coach to the darkly paneled room in which Lorry meets Lucie Manette, the opening chapters brim with gloomy corners and suggestive shadows.

These descriptions of darkness and secrets also contribute to the gothic atmosphere of the novel's opening. Gothic literature, a genre that establishes an uneasy, mysterious mood through the use of remote, desolate settings, supernatural or macabre events, and violence, dominated much of fiction from the late eighteenth century through the end of the nineteenth century. Such classics as *Frankenstein* (1818), by Mary Shelley, and *Wuthering Heights* (1847), by Emily Brontë, helped establish a strong tradition of gothic themes in British literature of this period. Jerry Cruncher's mysterious appearance during the treacherous nighttime journey, and Lorry's macabre visions of disinterring a body, hearken back to the eerie and supernatural feel of *A Tale of Two Cities'* gothic predecessors.

The obscurity that permeates these pages points to the "wonderful fact" that Dickens continuously ponders: every person in every room in every house that he passes possesses a secret, unknown to anyone—even closest friends, family, and lover. As the novel progresses, the reader witnesses Dickens digging—much as Lorry anticipates having to "dig" the doctor out of his ruinous prison experience—for the secrets that provide his characters with their essences and motivations.

In typical Dickensian manner, this project of discovery happens bit by bit: secrets emerge only very slowly. Although the horrible effects of Doctor Manette's incarceration become clear in the next few chapters, the reader doesn't learn the causes of these effects until the end of the novel. This narrative tactic owes much to the form in which Dickens wrote much of his work. *A Tale of Two Cities* was published as a serial piece—that is, in weekly installments from April 20 to November 26, 1859. The original serial format provides the reason for the novel's relatively short chapters and specific chapter subheadings, which, read in sequence, offer a skeletal outline of the plot. For example, the first three chapters of the second book bear the subheadings "Five Years Later," "A Sight," and "A Disappointment," respectively.

In addition to his plentiful literary talents, Dickens also possessed a shrewd businessman's sense. He remained keenly aware of what his reading public wanted and, unlike most artists of his caliber, unapologetically admitted to aiming for the largest possible readership. As he had done previously, with *A Tale of Two Cities,* Dickens set his sights on writing a so-called popular novel. One means of hooking readers into the story was to create a climate of suspense. Within the first four chapters, Dickens already leaves the reader with many questions that need to be answered, creating a sense of excitement and anticipation.

Book the First: Recalled to Life Chapters 5–6

Summary: Chapter 5: The Wine-shop

The wine was red wine, and had stained the ground of the narrow street. . . .

(See QUOTATIONS, *p. 61)*

The setting shifts from Dover, England to Saint Antoine, a poor suburb of Paris. A wine cask falls to the pavement in the street and everyone rushes to it. Men kneel and scoop up the wine that has pooled in the paving stones, while women sop up the liquid with handkerchiefs and wring them into the mouths of their babies. One man dips his finger into the "muddy wine-lees" and scrawls the word *blood* on a wall.

The wine shop is owned by Monsieur Defarge, a "bull-necked, martial-looking man of thirty." His wife, Madame Defarge, sits solemnly behind the counter, watchful of everything that goes on around her. She signals to her husband as he enters the wine shop, alerting him to the presence of an elderly gentleman and a young lady. Defarge eyes the strangers (they are Lorry and Lucie) but pretends not to notice them, speaking instead with three familiar customers, each of whom refers to the other two as "Jacques" (a code name that identifies themselves to one another as revolutionaries). After Defarge directs the men to a chamber on the fifth floor and sends them out, Mr. Lorry approaches from the corner and begs a word with Defarge. The men have a brief conversation, and soon Defarge leads Lorry and Lucie up a steep, dangerous rise of stairs. They come to a filthy landing, where the three men from the wine shop stand staring through chinks in the wall. Stating that he makes a show of Doctor Manette to a chosen few "to whom the sight is likely to do good," Defarge opens the door to reveal a white-haired man busily making shoes.

Chapter 6: The Shoemaker

Manette reports, in a voice gone faint with "solitude and disuse," that he is making a lady's shoe in the "present mode," or fashion, even though he has never seen the present fashion. When asked his name, he responds, "One Hundred and Five, North Tower." Lucie approaches. Noticing her radiant golden hair, Manette opens a knot of rag that he wears around his neck, in which he keeps a strand of similarly golden curls.

At first, Manette mistakes Lucie for his wife and recalls that, on the first day of his imprisonment, he begged to be allowed to keep these few stray hairs of his wife's as a means of escaping his circumstances "in the spirit." Lucie delivers an impassioned speech, imploring her father to weep if her voice or her hair recalls a loved one whom he once knew. She hints to him of the home that awaits him and assures him that his "agony is over." Manette collapses under a storm of emotion; Lucie urges that arrangements be made for his immediate departure for England. Fearing for Manette's health, Lorry protests, but Lucie insists that travel guarantees more safety than a continued stay in Paris. Defarge agrees and ushers the group into a coach.

ANALYSIS: CHAPTERS 5–6

In Chapters 5 and 6, Dickens introduces the reader to the first of the novel's two principal cities: Paris. The scramble for the leaking wine that opens "The Wine-shop" remains one of the most remembered (and frequently referenced) passages in the novel. In it, Dickens prepares the sweeping historical backdrop against which the tale of Lucie and Doctor Manette plays out. Although the French Revolution will not erupt for another fourteen years, the broken wine cask conveys the suffering and rage that will lead the French peasantry to revolt. The scene surrounding the wine cask contains a nightmarish quality. In clambering to feed on the dregs, the members of the mob stain themselves with wine. The liquid smears the peasants' hands, feet, and faces, foreshadowing the approaching chaos during which the blood of aristocrats and political dissidents will run as freely. The ominous scrawling of the word *blood* on the wall similarly prefigures the violence. Dickens here betrays his conflicted ideas regarding the revolution. While he acknowledges, throughout the novel, the horrible conditions that led the peasantry to violence, he never condones the peasants' actions. In his text the mob remains a frightening beast, manifesting a threat of danger rather than the promise of freedom: "Those who had been greedy with the staves of the cask, had acquired a tigerish smear about the mouth."

Dickens uses several techniques to criticize the corrupt circumstances of the peasants' oppression. He proves a master of irony and sarcasm, as becomes clear in his many biting commentaries; thus we read, "[France] entertained herself . . . with such humane achievements as sentencing a youth to have . . . his body burned alive" (Book the First, Chapter 1). Dickens also makes great use of anaphora, a rhetorical device wherein a word or phrase appears repeated in successive clauses or sentences. His meditation on hunger, which he cites as a defining impetus behind the peasants' imminent uprising, serves as a perfect example of how the author uses repetition to emphasize his point:

> Hunger was pushed out of the tall houses . . . Hunger
> was patched into them with straw and rag and wood and
> paper; Hunger was repeated in every fragment of the small
> modicum of firewood that the man sawed off; Hunger
> stared down the smokeless chimneys . . . Hunger was the
> inscription on the baker's shelves . . . Hunger rattled its dry
> bones among the roasting chestnuts in the turned cylinder;

*Hunger was shred into atomies in every farthing porringer
of husky chips of potato.... (Chapter 5)*

With this repetition, Dickens demonstrates that hunger dominates every aspect of these peasants' lives—they cannot do anything without being reminded of their hunger. The presence of the word *hunger* at the opening of each clause reflects the fact that hunger is the peasants' first thought and first word—they have no means to escape it. Reading the passage aloud, we become paralleled with the poor. We encounter "Hunger" at each breath.

In addition to setting the stage for revolution—both the historical upheaval in France and the more private but no less momentous changes in his characters' lives—Dickens establishes the unabashedly sentimental tone that characterizes many of the relationships in the novel, especially that between Doctor Manette and Lucie. As she coaxes her father into consciousness of his previous life and identity, Lucie emerges as a caricature of an innocent, pure-hearted, and loving woman. Most modern readers find her speech and gestures rather saccharine: "And if... I have to kneel to my honoured father, and implore his pardon for having never for his sake striven all day and lain awake and wept all night ... weep for it, weep for it!" Indeed, as a realistically imagined woman grieving over a family tragedy, Lucie proves unconvincing. Her emotions, her speech, and even her physical beauty belong to the realm of hyperbole. But Dickens does not aim for realism: he employs these sorts of exaggerations for the sake of emphasis and dramatic effect.

The Parisian revolutionaries first began addressing each of other as "Jacques" during the Jacquerie, a 1358 peasant uprising against French nobility. The nobles contemptuously referred to the peasants by the extremely common name of "Jacques" in order to accentuate their inferiority and deny their individuality. The peasants adopted the name as a war name. Just as the fourteenth-century peasants rallied around their shared low birth, so too do Dickens's revolutionaries fight as a unified machine of war. For example, at the storming of the Bastille in Book the Second, Chapter 21, Defarge cries out, "Work, comrades all, work! Work, Jacques One, Jacques Two, Jacques One Thousand, Jacques Two Thousand, Jacques Five-and-Twenty Thousand ... work!"

Book the Second: The Golden Thread
Chapters 1–4

Summary: Chapter 1: Five Years Later

It is now 1780. Tellson's Bank in London prides itself on being "very small, very dark, very ugly, very incommodious." Were it more welcoming, the bank's partners believe, it would lose its status as a respectable business. It is located by Temple Bar, the spot where, until recently, the government displayed the heads of executed criminals. The narrator explains that at this time, "death was a recipe much in vogue," used against all manner of criminals, from forgers to horse thieves to counterfeiters.

Jerry Cruncher, employed by Tellson's as a runner and messenger, wakes up in his small apartment, located in an unsavory London neighborhood. He begins the day by yelling at his wife for "praying against" him; he throws his muddy boot at her. Around nine o'clock, Cruncher and his young son camp outside Tellson's Bank, where they await the bankers' instructions. When an indoor messenger calls for a porter, Cruncher takes off to do the job. As young Jerry sits alone, he wonders why his father's fingers always have rust on them.

Summary: Chapter 2: A Sight

The bank clerk instructs Cruncher to go to the Old Bailey Courthouse and await orders from Jarvis Lorry. Cruncher arrives at the court, where Charles Darnay, a handsome, well-bred young man, stands trial for treason. Cruncher understands little of the legal jargon, but he gleans that Darnay has been charged with divulging secret information to the king of France (Louis XVI): namely, that England plans to send armed forces to fight in the American colonies. As Darnay looks to a young lady and her distinguished father, a whisper rushes through the courtroom, speculating on the identity of the two. Eventually, Cruncher discovers that they will serve as witnesses against the prisoner.

Summary: Chapter 3: A Disappointment

The Attorney-General prosecutes the case, demanding that the jury find Darnay guilty of passing English secrets into French hands. The Solicitor-General examines John Barsad, whose testimony supports the Attorney-General's case. The cross-examination, however, tarnishes Barsad's pure and righteous character. It reveals that he has served time in debtor's prison and has been involved in brawls over gambling. The prosecution calls its next witness, Roger Cly, whom the defense attorney, Mr. Stryver, also exposes as a dubious, untrustworthy witness. Mr. Lorry then takes the stand, and the prosecution asks him if, five years ago, he shared a Dover mail coach with the accused. Lorry contends that his fellow passengers sat so bundled up that their identities remained hidden. The prosecutors then ask similar questions of Lucie, the young woman Darnay had noticed earlier. She admits to meeting the prisoner on the ship back to England. When she recounts how he helped her to care for her sick father, however, she seems to help his case—yet she then inadvertently turns the court against Darnay by reporting his statement that George Washington's fame might one day match that of George III. Doctor Manette is also called to the stand, but he claims that he remembers nothing of the trip due to his illness.

Mr. Stryver is in the middle of cross-examining another witness "with no result" when his insolent young colleague, Sydney Carton, passes him a note. Stryver begins arguing the contents of the note, which draws the court's attention to Carton's own uncanny resemblance to the prisoner. The undeniable likeness foils the court's ability to identify Darnay as a spy beyond reasonable doubt. The jury retires to deliberate and eventually returns with an acquittal for Darnay.

Summary: Chapter 4: Congratulatory

Doctor Manette, Lucie, Mr. Lorry, Mr. Stryver, and Darnay exit the courtroom. The narrator relates that Manette has established himself as an upright and distinguished citizen, though the gloom of his terrible past descends on him from time to time. These clouds descend only rarely, however, and Lucie feels confident in her power as the "golden thread" that unites him to a past and present "beyond his misery." Darnay kisses Lucie's hand and then turns to Stryver to thank him for his work. Lucie, Manette, and Stryver depart, and a drunk Sydney Carton emerges from the shadows to join the men. Lorry chastises him for not being a serious man of business. Darnay and Carton make their way to a tavern, where Carton smugly asks, "Is it worth being tried for one's life, to be the object of [Lucie's] sympathy and compassion . . . ?" When Darnay comments that Carton has been drinking, Carton gives his reason for indulging himself so: "I am a disappointed drudge, sir. I care for no man on earth, and no man on earth cares for me." After Darnay leaves,

Carton curses his own image in the mirror, as well as his look-alike, who reminds him of what he has "fallen away from."

ANALYSIS: CHAPTERS 1–4

The courtroom scenes that open the second book of the novel allow Dickens to use a wonderful range of language. He employs a technique known as free indirect style, which fuses third-person narration with an interior point of view. He reveals the charges for which Darnay is being tried while rooting the reader in the uneducated mind (and ear) of the spectators: "Charles Darnay had yesterday pleaded Not Guilty to an indictment denouncing him (with infinite jingle and jangle) for that he was a false traitor to our serene, illustrious, excellent, and so forth, prince. . . ." The juxtaposition of formal ("our serene, illustrious, excellent") and informal ("and so forth") speech produces a comical effect by highlighting the unrefined crowd's zealous craving for the juicy details of the case, even as they recognize the decorum of their setting.

Dickens also uses these scenes to implement another of his favorite literary devices, parody. The Attorney-General's long, self-important, and bombastic speech at the opening of Chapter 3 offers a highly comical imitation of legalese and serves indirectly to ridicule the Attorney-General, as well as the entire legal system. Thus the Attorney-General's informs the jury:

> [I]f statues were decreed in Britain, as in ancient Greece and Rome, to public benefactors, this shining citizen [his witness] would assuredly have one. That, as they were not so decreed, he probably would not have one.

The Attorney-General melodramatically touts the virtues of his witness, John Barsad, and absurdly deifies him, as though Barsad were a great figure from antiquity. When he explains that Barsad would not in fact have such a statue erected in his honor, as no such practice exists in England, his words again produce a comical effect. They draw attention to the fact that the attorney's first sentence glorified Barsad to the point of irrelevant hypotheticals. Moreover, the redundant nature of the Attorney-General's statement highlights his obliviousness to the emptiness of his words.

The passage makes clear how Dickens's comical characterizations have won him the admiration of generations of readers. *A Tale of Two Cities,* however, is far from a comic novel; and perhaps in withholding humor from the book, Dickens sacrificed some opportunity to put his greatest talents to work. Dickens's most "Dickensian" novels abound with hilariously grotesque characters, whose speech (usually vulgar) and appearance (usually freakish) are rendered with extreme exaggeration. With his impeded speech, violent temper, mysteriously rusty fingers, and muddy boots, Jerry Cruncher comes as close as any other character to this sort of caricature. But with A Tale of Two Cities, Dickens was making a conscious decision to steer away from his trademark characters, in order to write a novel in shorter and more frequent installments than usual. He determined to strip the story of dialogue, upon which he often relied to flesh out his characters and further his narration, in favor of describing the story's action. By shifting his attention from character to plot, Dickens crafted A Tale of Two Cities into a rather un-Dickensian novel. His biographer, John Forster, doubted the benefits of such a move:

> To rely less upon character than upon incident, and to resolve that his actors should be expressed by the story more than they should express themselves by dialogue, was for him a hazardous, and can hardly be called an entirely successful, experiment.

As Charles Darnay and Sydney Carton take the stage in this section, Forster's comment becomes particularly pertinent. Darnay makes as uninteresting a hero as Lucie does a heroine. Both characters prove rather one-dimensional in their goodness and virtue. Only the supposedly loveless Carton promises more depth. He descends into the darkness of alcoholism while others bask in the glow of Darnay's acquittal. Reading of this, one cannot help but suspect that elaborate secrets dim his past.

Book the Second: The Golden Thread
Chapters 5–6

Summary: Chapter 5: The Jackal
Sydney Carton, the "idlest and most unpromising of men," makes his way from the tavern to Mr. Stryver's apartment. The men drink together and discuss the day's court proceedings. Stryver, nicknamed "the lion," compliments his friend, "the jackal," for the "rare point" that he made regarding Darnay's identification. However, he laments Carton's moodiness. Ever since their days in school together, Stryver observes, Carton has fluctuated between highs and

lows, "now in spirits and now in despondency!" Carton shrugs off Stryver's accusation that his life lacks a unified direction. Unable to match Stryver's vaulting ambition, Carton claims that he has no other choice but to live his life "in rust and repose." Attempting to change the subject, Stryver turns the conversation to Lucie, praising her beauty. Carton dismisses her as a "golden-haired doll," but Stryver wonders about Carton's true feelings for her.

SUMMARY: CHAPTER 6: HUNDREDS OF PEOPLE

Four months later, Mr. Lorry, now a trusted friend of the Manette family, arrives at Doctor Manette's home. Finding Manette and his daughter not at home, he converses with Miss Pross. They discuss why the doctor continues to keep his shoemaker's bench.

Their conversation also touches on the number of suitors who come to call on Lucie. Miss Pross complains that they come by the dozen, by the hundred—all "people who are not at all worthy of Ladybird." In Miss Pross's opinion, the only man worthy of Lucie is her own brother, Solomon Pross, who, she laments, disqualified himself by making a certain mistake. Lorry knows, however, that Solomon is a scoundrel who robbed Miss Pross of her possessions and left her in poverty. He goes on to ask if Manette ever returns to his shoemaking, and Pross assures him that the doctor no longer thinks about his dreadful imprisonment.

Lucie and Manette return, and soon Darnay joins them. Darnay relates that a workman, making alterations to a cell in the Tower of London, came upon a carving in the wall: "D I G." At first, the man mistook these for some prisoner's initials, but he soon enough realized that they spelled the word *dig*. Upon digging, the man discovered the ashes of a scrap of paper on which the prisoner must have written a message. The story startles Manette, but he soon recovers.

Carton arrives and sits with the others near a window in the drawing room. The footsteps on the street below make a terrific echo. Lucie imagines that the footsteps belong to people that will eventually enter into their lives. Carton comments that if Lucie's speculation is true, then a great crowd must be on its way.

ANALYSIS: CHAPTERS 5–6

Dickens devotes Chapter 5 to the character of Sydney Carton, whom he nicknames "the jackal." Given the secondary meaning of the term—an accomplice in the commission of menial or disreputable acts—the name seems fitting. Alongside his colleague Stryver,

Carton seems little more than an assistant. He lacks ambition; in the courtroom he spends his time staring at the ceiling; outside of it, he spends his time getting drunk. Carton accepts his pathetic state—he says to Stryver matter-of-factly, "you have fallen into your rank, and I have fallen into mine." Yet, for all of his supposed indifference, he betrays his desire for a better, more exalted life. Carton alludes several times to the respectable life that he might have lived. At the end of Chapter 4, he admits to hating Darnay because the man reminds him of what he could have been. He echoes this sentiment in Chapter 5, telling Stryver, "I thought I should have been much the same sort of fellow [as Darnay], if I had had any luck." These feelings evidence his resentful awareness of Darnay as his double—a successful and happy double, and thus a mocking one. Carton views Darnay as a concrete manifestation of a life he might have led, a life preferable to his own. The closing of the chapter alludes to the secret longings of a man who will not admit to having any:

> In the fair city of this vision, there were airy galleries from which the loves and graces looked upon him, gardens in which the fruits of life hung ripening, waters of Hope that sparkled in his sight. A moment, and it was gone. Climbing to a high chamber in a well of houses, he threw himself down in his clothes on a neglected bed, and its pillow was wet with wasted tears.

A great gulf exists between the life that Carton leads and the life that he imagines for himself, between the type of man that he is and the type of man that he dreams of being. Carton's complex and conflicted inner life paves the way for his dramatic development, which eventually elevates him out of his jackal status.

Dickens employs masterful foreshadowing in Chapter 6, as he uses these scenes both to hint at Carton's eventual ascendance into glory and to anticipate two vital plot turns. The discovery of the mysterious letter in the Tower of London, and Manette's distress upon hearing of it, foreshadows the moment when, during a later trial, the prosecution will confront the doctor with a letter he wrote while imprisoned in the Bastille. As the second trial forms the dramatic core of the latter half of the novel, the discovery of this second letter forms a crucial part of the plot and dictates the course of the characters' lives. By introducing the story of a first and parallel letter, Dickens prepares the reader for the discovery of the second. As soon as the second letter surfaces, the reader will instantly recognize it as important. The second event that Dickens foreshadows is the French Revolution itself. The "hundreds of people" to which the title of Chapter 6 owes its name refers not to Lucie's suitors (whose numbers Miss Pross clearly exaggerates) but to the multitude of angry, mutinous revolutionaries who, as Lucie and Carton foretell, will soon march into the characters' lives.

BOOK THE SECOND: THE GOLDEN THREAD CHAPTERS 7–9

SUMMARY: CHAPTER 7: MONSEIGNEUR IN TOWN

Monseigneur, a great lord in the royal court, holds a reception in Paris. He surrounds himself with the greatest pomp and luxury. For example, he has four serving men help him drink his chocolate. The narrator tells us that Monseigneur's money corrupts everyone who touches it. Monseigneur parades around his guests briefly and then returns to his sanctuary. Miffed at Monseigneur's haughtiness, one guest, the Marquis Evrémonde, condemns Monseigneur as he leaves. The Marquis orders his carriage to be raced through the city streets, delighting to see the commoners nearly run down by his horses. Suddenly the carriage jolts to a stop. A child lies dead under its wheels. The Marquis tosses a few coins to the boy's father, a man named Gaspard, and to the wine-shop owner Defarge, who tries to comfort Gaspard. As the Marquis drives away, a coin comes flying back into the carriage, thrown in bitterness. He curses the commoners, saying that he would willingly ride over any of them. Madame Defarge watches the scene, knitting the entire time.

CHAPTER 8: MONSEIGNEUR IN THE COUNTRY

The Marquis arrives in the small village to which he serves as lord. There, too, the people live wretched lives, exploited, poor, and starving. As he looks over the submissive faces of the peasants, he singles out a road-mender whom he passed on his journey, a man whose fixed stare bothered him. He demands to know what the road-mender was staring at, and the man responds that someone was holding onto the bottom of the carriage. The Marquis continues on his way and soon comes upon a peasant woman, mourning at a rustic graveside. The woman stops him and begs that he provide her husband's grave with some stone or marker, lest he be forgotten, but the Marquis drives away, unmoved. He arrives at his chateau and, upon entering, asks if Monsieur Charles has arrived from England.

CHAPTER 9: THE GORGON'S HEAD

Later that night, at the Marquis' chateau, Charles Darnay, the nephew of the Marquis, arrives by carriage. Darnay tells his uncle that he wants to renounce the title and property that he stands to inherit when the Marquis dies. The family's name, Darnay contends, is associated with "fear and slavery." He insists that the family has consistently acted shamefully, "injuring every human creature who came between us and our pleasure." The Marquis dismisses these protests, urging his nephew to accept his "natural destiny." The next morning, the Marquis is found dead with a knife through his heart. Attached to the knife is a note that reads: "Drive him fast to his tomb. This, from Jacques."

ANALYSIS: CHAPTERS 7–9

In Chapter 5 of Book the First, we read a description of the French public squabbling over the spilled contents of a broken wine cask; this passage, in its indictment of the greed and viciousness of the mob, forms the backbone of Dickens's criticism against the impending revolution. In this section, in contrast, Dickens expresses an equal disapproval for the aristocracy whose vile mistreatment of the peasantry contributes to the revolution. Again, Dickens uses sarcasm to great effect as he describes the Monseigneur's ridiculous dependence on his serving men:

> It was impossible for Monseigneur to dispense with
> one of these attendants on the chocolate and hold his
> high place under the admiring Heavens. Deep would
> have been the blot upon his escutcheon if his chocolate
> had been ignobly waited on by only three men; he must
> have died of two.

Dickens's choice of the word *escutcheon*, referring to a family coat-of-arms, is key to our understanding of Monseigneur. For this emblem represents what the he sees as a power inherent to his family's bloodline, an innate nobility that he thinks justifies his absurd lavishness. Dickens undercuts Monseigneur's reverence for this symbol of his own power by commenting on his ridiculous fear that he might damage his reputation should he prove insufficiently ostentatious in the frivolous act of drinking chocolate. Moreover, in noting Monseigneur's deep interest in the ritual of imbibing his little treat, Dickens contrasts him with the more loftily motivated characters in the novel. While the novel's worthy characters act according to selfless and righteous goals, the Monseigneur conducts himself according to base and earthly instincts.

Dickens uses the Marquis Evrémonde to give a similar portrait of the aristocracy as elitist. The Marquis displays no sympathy for Gaspard, the father of the boy whom his carriage crushes. Rather, he believes that his noble blood justifies his malicious treatment of his plebian subjects. In tossing the coins to Gaspard, he aims to buy his way out of the predicament and rid his own conscience of the nuisance of Gaspard's grief. He believes that it is the commoner's lot in life to struggle and suffer. Likewise, he has no doubt that his nephew's rightful station is to dominate commoners, referring to his nephew's noble blood as his "natural destiny."

Dickens sets up the Marquis as a representative of the French aristocracy and, as such, a direct cause of the imminent revolution. Using a device called personification, he creates human manifestations of such abstract concepts as greed, oppression, and hatred. The Marquis, so exaggeratedly cruel and flamboyant, hardly seems an actual human being—hardly a realistic character. Instead, the Marquis stands as a symbol or personification of the "inhuman abandonment of consideration" endemic to the French aristocracy during the eighteenth century.

Dickens advances this impression of the Marquis's character in the opening passage of Chapter 9, when he describes the nobleman's chateau:

> It was a heavy mass of building, that chateau of Monsieur
> the Marquis, with a large stone court-yard before it, and
> two stone sweeps of staircase meeting in a stone terrace
> before the principal door. A stony business altogether
> with heavy stone balustrades . . . and stone faces of
> men, and stone heads of lions, in all directions. As if the
> Gorgon's head had surveyed it, when it was finished, two
> centuries ago.

The repetition of the word *stone* solidifies, as it were, our impression of the man who lives in the chateau. His heart, Dickens suggests, possesses the same severity as the castle's walls. The mention of the Gorgon—one of three Greek mythological sisters who had snakes for hair and turned anyone who looked at them to stone—foreshadows the death of the Marquis. For by the end of the chapter, the chateau has one more stone face added to its collection—the dead Marquis's face, which the narrator describes as "like a stone mask, suddenly startled, made angry, and petrified." Lying dead on his pillow, the Marquis serves as a warning of the violence and bloodshed to come, initiated by the masses who can no longer abide the aristocracy's heartless oppression of them.

BOOK THE SECOND: THE GOLDEN THREAD CHAPTERS 10–13

SUMMARY: CHAPTER 10: TWO PROMISES
A year later, Darnay makes a moderate living as a French teacher in London. He visits Doctor Manette and admits his love for Lucie. He honors Manette's special relationship with his daughter, assuring him that his own love for Lucie will in no way disturb that bond. Manette applauds Darnay for speaking so "feelingly and so manfully" and asks if he seeks a promise from him. Darnay asks Manette to promise to vouch for what he has said, for the true nature of his love, should Lucie ever ask. Manette promises as much. Wanting to be worthy of his confidence, Darnay attempts to tell Manette his real name, confessing that it is not Darnay. Manette stops him short, making him promise to reveal his name only if he proves successful in his courtship. He will hear Darnay's secret on his wedding day. Hours later, after Darnay has left, Lucie hears her father cobbling away at his shoemaker's bench. Frightened by his relapse, she watches him as he sleeps that night.

SUMMARY: CHAPTER 11: A COMPANION PICTURE
Late that same night, Carton and Stryver work in Stryver's chambers. In his puffed-up and arrogant manner, Stryver announces that he intends to marry Lucie. Carton drinks heavily at the news, assuring Stryver that his words have not upset him. Stryver suggests that Carton himself find "some respectable woman with a little property," and marry her, lest he end up ill and penniless.

SUMMARY: CHAPTER 12: THE FELLOW OF DELICACY
The next day, Stryver plans to take Lucie to the Vauxhall Gardens to make his marriage proposal. On his way, he drops in at Tellson's Bank, where he informs Mr. Lorry of his intentions. Lorry persuades Stryver to postpone his proposal until he knows for certain that Lucie will accept. This admonition upsets Stryver. He almost insults Lucie as a "mincing Fool," but Lorry warns him against doing so. Lorry asks that Stryver hold off his proposal for a few hours to give him time to consult the family and see exactly where Stryver stands.

Later that night, Lorry visits Stryver and reports that his fears have been confirmed. If Stryver were to propose, the Manettes would reject his offer. Stryver dismisses the entire affair as one of the "vanities" of "empty-headed girls" and begs Lorry to forget it.

SUMMARY: CHAPTER 13: THE FELLOW OF NO DELICACY

Carton, who frequently wanders near the Manettes' house late at night, enters the house one August day and speaks to Lucie alone. She observes a change in his face. He laments his wasted life, despairing that he shall never live a better life than the one he now lives. Lucie assures him that he might become much worthier of himself. She believes that her tenderness can save him. Carton insists that he has declined beyond salvation but admits that he has always viewed Lucie as "the last dream of [his] soul." She has made him consider beginning his life again, though he no longer believes in the possibility of doing so. He feels happy to have admitted this much to Lucie and to know that something remains in him that still deserves pity. Carton ends his confession with a pledge that he would do anything for Lucie, including give his life.

ANALYSIS: CHAPTERS 10–13

In this section, Dickens develops the love triangle among Lucie, Carton, and Darnay. Rather than simply writing an encyclopedic account of the French Revolution, Dickens balances history with the more private struggles of his principal characters. He links the two sides of his novel thematically, as each raises questions about the possibilities of revolution and resurrection—Carton, for example, like France itself, strikes out for a new life.

It is in Chapter 13 that Dickens lays the foundation for Carton's eventual turnaround. Upon seeing Carton, Lucie observes a change in his demeanor. Much of this change owes to Carton's feelings for her. Just as Carton shares Darnay's physical countenance, he also shares Darnay's devotion to Lucie. Yet Carton's confession strikes the reader as more touching and profound than that of his counterpart. The reader certainly believes Darnay as he informs Manette, "Dear Doctor Manette, I love your daughter fondly, dearly, disinterestedly, devotedly. If ever there were love in the world, I love her," but this declaration, while direct, seems rather vapid and unimaginative. The alliteration of "dearly, disinterestedly, devotedly" highlights the flat—almost bored—tone of the declaration as it slogs through its sequence of adverbs. The closing sentence seems almost a parody of Romantic love poetry. Darnay touts his love as a great force of the universe but does so with the most mundane possible phrasing, and the repetition of the word *love* is dogged and uninspired.

Carton's words, on the other hand, betray a deep psychological and emotional struggle, suggesting the existence of feelings more complex, perhaps even more worthy of reciprocation, than Darnay's:

> *In my degradation I have not been so degraded but*
> *that the sight of you with your father, and of this home*
> *made such a home by you, has stirred old shadows that*
> *I thought had died out of me. . . . I have had unformed*
> *ideas of striving afresh, beginning anew, shaking off sloth*
> *and sensuality, and fighting out the abandoned fight.*

In his depiction of his love, Carton opens himself to the reader's sympathy in a way that Darnay does not. Whereas Darnay makes an objective, almost factual statement of his love for Lucie, Carton describes his emotions, tinged as they are by realistic insecurity ("my degradation") and uncertainty ("unformed ideas"). He also speaks poetically of "old shadows" and "the abandoned fight"; his use of metaphor seems to reflect his inability to grasp fully his profound feelings. Darnay, in contrast, categorizes his experience simply as "love," not pausing to ponder the emotions behind the word.

Lucie's conjecture on whether she can "recall [Carton] . . . to a better course" echoes the beginning of the novel, when Lorry recalls Doctor Manette to life. Manette had to suffer a death of sorts—wasting nearly twenty years in prison—before being reborn into the life of love and devotion with Lucie. Now, Carton, too, shall have to undergo a sort of death or sacrifice in order to win the fight for love and meaning that he claims to have abandoned.

Dickens's characteristic humor, largely absent from *A Tale of Two Cities,* shines through in his depiction of Stryver in Chapter 12. Dickens uses Stryver's name to suggest the essential nature of his character. Coldly ambitious, the man ruthlessly strives to distinguish himself as a great businessman and here, in Chapter 12, endeavors to win the hand of Lucie Manette. Dickens ironically entitles the chapter "The Fellow of Delicacy," bringing Stryver's coarseness into greater relief. In Stryver's surly refusal to heed Lorry's gentle advice and postpone his courtship of Lucie, we see clearly one of Dickens's greatest talents—the ability to capture a character through dialogue.

> *"Were you going [to Lucie's] now?" asked Mr. Lorry.*
> *"Straight!" said Stryver, with a plump of his fist on the desk.*
> *"Then I think I wouldn't, if I was you."*
> *"Why?" said Stryver. "Now, I'll put you in a corner,"* forensically shaking a forefinger at him. "You are a man of business and bound to have a reason. State your reason. Why wouldn't you go?"*

The directness of Stryver's response to Lorry ("Straight!") and the emphatic nature of his accompanying thump on the table demonstrate his blind and unshakeable ambition. His finger-wagging and blustery imperative demanding to hear Lorry's "reason" reveal his aggressive nature and refusal to be hindered in his pursuits. In his interrogating and intimidating mannerisms, Stryver acts as if he were arguing a legal point or cross-examining a witness. It is clear to the reader that he approaches the courtship as he would a case in court—as a way to gain money and stature—and not out of fondness for Lucie.

BOOK THE SECOND: THE GOLDEN THREAD
CHAPTERS 14–17

SUMMARY: CHAPTER 14: THE HONEST TRADESMAN

One morning outside Tellson's Bank, Jerry Cruncher sees a funeral pass by. Jerry asks a few questions and learns that the crowd is preparing to bury Roger Cly, a convicted spy and one of the men who testified against Darnay in his court case. Cruncher joins the motley procession, which includes a chimney-sweep, a bear-leader and his mangy bear, and a pieman. After much drinking and carousing, the mob buries Cly and, for sport, decides to accuse passersby of espionage in order to wreak "vengeance on them." At home that night, Cruncher once again harangues his wife for her prayers. He then announces that he is going "fishing." In reality, he goes to dig up Cly's body in order to sell it to scientists. Unbeknownst to Cruncher, his son follows him to the cemetery, but runs away terrified, believing that the coffin is chasing him. The next day, he asks his father the definition of a "Resurrection-Man"—the term describes men like Cruncher, who dig up bodies to sell to science. He announces his intentions to have this job as an adult.

SUMMARY: CHAPTER 15: KNITTING

In Paris, Defarge enters his wine shop with a mender of roads whom he calls "Jacques." Three men file out of the shop individually. Eventually, Defarge and the mender of roads climb up to the garret where Doctor Manette had been hidden. There they join the three men who recently exited the shop, and whom Defarge also calls "Jacques." The mender of roads reports that, a year ago, he saw a man hanging by a chain underneath the Marquis' carriage. Several months later, he says, he saw the man again, being marched along the road by soldiers. The soldiers led the man to prison, where he remained "in his iron cage" for several days. Accused of killing the Marquis, he stood to be executed as a parricide (one who murders a close relative). According to rumor, petitions soon arrived in Paris begging that the prisoner's life be spared. However, workmen built a gallows in the middle of town, and soon the man was hanged.

When the mender of roads finishes his recollection, Defarge asks him to wait outside a moment. The other Jacques call for the extermination of the entire aristocracy. One points to the knitting work of Madame Defarge, which, in its stitching, contains an elaborate registry of the names of those whom the revolutionaries aim to kill. He asks if the woman will always be able to decipher the names that appear there. Later that week, Defarge and his wife take the mender of roads to Versailles to see King Louis XVI and Queen Marie Antoinette. When the royal couple appears, the mender of roads cries "Long live the King!" and becomes so excited that Defarge must "restrain him from flying at the objects of his brief devotion and tearing them to pieces." This performance pleases the Defarges, who see that their efforts will prove easier if the aristocrats continue to believe in the peasantry's allegiance.

SUMMARY: CHAPTER 16: STILL KNITTING

The Defarges return to Saint Antoine later that evening. A policeman friend warns Defarge that a spy by the name of John Barsad has been sent to their neighborhood. Madame Defarge resolves to knit his name into the register. That night, Defarge admits his fear that the revolution will not come in his lifetime. Madame Defarge dismisses his impatience and compares the revolution to lightning and an earthquake: it strikes quickly and with great force, but no one knows how long it will take to form. The next day, Barsad visits the wine shop. He masquerades as a sympathizer with the revolutionaries and comments on the horrible treatment of the peasants. Knowing that Defarge once worked as Doctor Manette's servant, he reports that Lucie Manette plans to marry, and that her husband is to be the Marquis' nephew, Darnay. After Barsad leaves, Madame Defarge adds Darnay's name to her registry, unsettling Defarge, the once loyal servant of Manette.

SUMMARY: CHAPTER 17: ONE NIGHT

It is the eve of Lucie's marriage to Darnay. Lucie and her father have enjoyed long days of happiness together. Doctor Manette finally has begun to put his imprisonment behind him. For the first time since his release, Manette speaks of his days in the Bastille. In prison, he passed much time imagining what sort of person Lucie would grow up to be. He is very happy now, thanks to Lucie, who has brought him "consolation and restoration." Later that night, Lucie sneaks down to her father's room and finds him sleeping soundly.

ANALYSIS: CHAPTERS 14–17

Of the many shadows throughout the novel, that of death looms most largely. Given the novel's concern with resurrection, death acquires an inevitable presence. Although young Jerry Cruncher's aborted trip to the cemetery at the heels of his grave-robbing father serves little dramatic purpose, it functions as an important tableau. As the boy runs home with visions in his head of Roger Cly's coffin chasing behind him, Dickens creates a suggestive symbol of the death that overshadows and pursues everyone.

As critic G. Robert Stange has noted, "the tableau technique" plays an important role in the novel. "Dickens tends throughout to make important episodes into set-pieces that are more visual than strictly dramatic." Chapter 14 opens with such a tableau—that of Cly's funeral scene. In the scene's emphasis on bizarre and freakish imagery, we see a clear example of Dickens's characteristic sense of the grotesque. The scene's importance also lies in its depiction of the throng attending Cly's funeral. Here, Dickens continues his criticism of mob mentality. Although Dickens intends the scene as largely comic, he also prepares the reader for his later, darker scenes of mindless frenzy and group violence in Paris. For example, as Cruncher participates in the burial of a man he does not know, his spirited condemnation of the deceased testifies to the contagious nature of the crowd's anger and excitement. Indeed, once the body is interred, the mob's energy remains unexhausted. Thus the group sets off to harass casual passers-by. Dickens later taps into the same frightening group psychology in the tableau that portray the French revolutionaries as they gather around the grindstone (in Book the Third, Chapter 2) and dance the Carmagnole (in Book the Third, Chapter 5).

The comedic atmosphere effected by Cruncher quickly lapses into a tone of ominous danger as the story comes to focus on Madame Defarge. For this woman possesses a vengeance and hatred that exceed all bounds. Indeed, the preceding scene presages her vindictive nature: the funeral-goers' boisterous accusations of espionage against innocent passers-by, which they voice for the sake of "vengeance," foreshadow the sweeping tide of hatred that consumes the revolutionaries, and Madame Defarge in particular. Two of the chapters in this section center around her knitting, her symbolic hatred of the aristocracy. When one of the Jacques inquires as to whether Madame Defarge will always be able to decipher this register, his query presages a time in which the woman will seek death even for those objectively innocent of any oppressive behaviors, a time in which her monomaniacal bloodlust will drive her to murder without heed of her scrupulous register.

Dickens derived his knitting motif from historical record: many scholars have recorded that women of the period would often knit as they stood and watched the daily executions. In the hands of Madame Defarge, however, the pastime takes on symbolic significance. In Greek mythology, the Fates were three sisters who controlled human life: one sister spun the web of life, one measured it, and the last cut it. Dickens employs a similar metaphor. As Madame Defarge weaves the names of the condemned into shrouds, her knitting becomes a symbol of her victims' fate, their death at the hands of a vengeful peasantry.

BOOK THE SECOND: THE GOLDEN THREAD CHAPTERS 18–21

SUMMARY: CHAPTER 18: NINE DAYS

Darnay and Doctor Manette converse before going to church for Darnay's wedding to Lucie. Manette emerges "deadly pale" from this meeting. Darnay and Lucie are married and depart for their honeymoon. Almost immediately, a change comes over Manette; he now looks scared and lost. Later that day, Miss Pross and Mr. Lorry discover Manette at his shoemaker's bench, lapsed into an incoherent state. They fear that he will not recover in time to join the

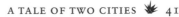

newlyweds, as planned, on the honeymoon, and for nine days they keep careful watch over him.

SUMMARY: CHAPTER 19: AN OPINION

On the tenth morning, Lorry wakes to find the shoemaker's bench put away and the Doctor reading a book. Lorry cautiously asks Manette what might have caused the now-ended relapse, relating Manette's strange case as though it had happened to someone else. Manette suggests that he himself anticipated the reversion. He goes on to say that some stimulus must have triggered a memory strong enough to cause it. Manette reassures Miss Pross and Lorry that such a relapse is not likely to recur because the circumstances that caused it are unlikely to surface again. Still speaking as though the afflicted party were someone other than Manette, Lorry creates a scenario about a blacksmith. He asks whether, if the smith's forge were associated with a trauma, the smith's tools should be taken from him in order to spare him painful memories. Manette answers that the man used those tools to comfort his tortured mind and should be allowed to keep them. Eventually, however, Manette agrees, for Lucie's sake, to let Lorry dispose of his tools while he is away. A few days later, Manette leaves to join Lucie and Darnay. In his absence, Lorry and Miss Pross hack the shoemaker's bench to pieces, burn it, and bury the tools.

SUMMARY: CHAPTER 20: A PLEA

When Lucie and Darnay return home from their honeymoon, Sydney Carton is their first visitor. He apologizes for his drunkenness on the night of the trial and delivers a self-effacing speech in which he asks for Darnay's friendship: "If you could endure to have such a worthless fellow . . . coming and going at odd times, I should ask that I might be permitted to come and go as a privileged person [in the household]. . . ." Carton leaves. Afterward, Darnay comments that Carton tends to be careless and reckless. Lucie deems this judgment too harsh and insists that Carton possesses a good, though wounded, heart. Lucie's compassion touches Darnay, and he promises to regard Carton's faults with sympathy.

SUMMARY: CHAPTER 21: ECHOING FOOTSTEPS

Years go by, and Lucie and her family enjoy a tranquil life. She gives birth to a daughter, little Lucie, and a son, who dies young. Lucie still maintains her habit of sitting in a corner of the parlor, listening to the echoing footsteps on the street below. By 1789, the echoes reverberate "from a distance" and make a sound "as of a great storm in France with a dreadful sea rising." One day in July, Lorry visits the Darnays and reports that an alarming number of French citizens are sending their money and property to England.

The scene then shifts to the storming of the Bastille in Paris. Defarge and Madame Defarge serve as leaders among the mob. Once inside the Bastille, Defarge grabs a guard and demands to be taken to 105 North Tower. Defarge searches the cell. When he is finished, he rejoins the mob as it murders and mutilates the governor who had defended the fortress. Madame Defarge cuts off the man's head.

ANALYSIS: CHAPTERS 18–21

Nearly every character in the novel battles against some form of imprisonment. In the case of Doctor Manette and Charles Darnay, this imprisonment is quite literal. But subtler, psychological confines torture other characters as much as any stone cell. Sydney Carton, for instance, cannot seem to escape his listlessness. Darnay struggles to free himself from the legacy of his family history. Lorry tries to unshackle his heart from its enslavement to Tellson's Bank. Finally, although Manette long ago escaped the Bastille, in this section he battles the tormenting memories of his years there. Prompted by the discovery of Darnay's true identity, Manette reverts to pounding out shoes in order to calm his troubled mind. This episode brings the notion of the fight for freedom from the level of political revolution to the level of personal struggles, suggesting that men and women toil to free themselves from the forces that oppress them as surely as nations do.

Dickens further elaborates the parallel between personal and public struggles in Chapter 21, which begins with Lucie in her parlor listening to the echo of footsteps on the street, and then shifts to the storming of the Bastille in Paris. The footsteps sweep the reader along, from the intimate struggles of private life to a revolution that will shape the future of an entire country and continent. Dickens's description of the battle contains exceptional power. Consider the following passage from Chapter 21:

> *Flashing weapons, blazing torches, smoking waggon-loads*
> *of wet straw, hard work at neighbouring barricades in all*
> *directions, shrieks, volleys, execrations, bravery without*
> *stint, boom, smash and rattle, and the furious sounding*
> *of the living sea; but, still the deep ditch, and the single*

> *drawbridge, and the massive stone walls, and the eight*
> *great towers, and still Defarge of the wine-shop at his gun,*
> *grown doubly hot by the service of Four fierce hours.*

Here Dickens captures the frantic and dangerous energy of the conflict. This passage's effect owes much to Dickens's language, which employs both alliteration and onomatopoeia to evoke the mood of battle. Alliteration, or the repetition of consonants, fills the passage with harsh sounds. The effect, in the last line for instance, mimics the regular bursts of gunfire: "at his *gun, grown* doubly hot by the service of *Four fierce* hours" (emphasis added). The passage's onomatopoeia, or use of words that imitate the sound to which they refer—such as *boom, smash,* and *rattle*—contributes to the overall impression of chaos as the sounds of the battle take over. Both methods cause an abstract description to give way to an eruption of noise, as the harsh and relentless pounding and battering of the siege becomes a palpable presence in the text.

As the battle rages on, Dickens introduces a symbol that plays a major role in the novel's theme of resurrection: blood, which begins to flow in the streets of Saint Antoine. Dickens links the image of blood to that of wine: after a day of butchery, the revolutionaries' clothes and hands bear stains of red, recalling the day on which the wine cask breaks in front of Defarge's shop (Book the First, Chapter 5). With these allegorical images of blood and wine, the theme of resurrection takes on a decidedly Christian undertone. In the Catholic ritual of communion, the priest consecrates a cup of wine and it becomes the blood of Christ, whose entombment and miraculous ascent to heaven on Easter Day have rendered him a symbol of resurrection in Christian tradition. In later chapters, Dickens will continue to draw upon this Christian association of blood, wine, and resurrection. Just as Christ shed his wine red blood upon the cross prior to being entombed and resurrected, so must the blood of the aristocracy flow before the commoners can take up their new lives.

BOOK THE SECOND: THE GOLDEN THREAD CHAPTERS 22–24

SUMMARY: CHAPTER 22: THE SEA STILL RISES
One week later in Saint Antoine, Defarge arrives bearing news of the capture of Foulon, a wealthy man who once declared that if people were starving they should eat grass. Foulon had faked his

own death to avoid the peasants' fury but was later discovered hiding in the country. The revolutionaries set out to meet Foulon, led by Madame Defarge and a woman known only as The Vengeance. The mob strings Foulon up, but the rope breaks and he does not die until his third hanging. The peasants put his head on a pike and fill his mouth with grass. When they have finished, the peasants eat their "scanty and insufficient suppers," parents play with their children, and lovers love.

SUMMARY: CHAPTER 23: FIRE RISES
The French countryside lies ruined and desolate. An unidentified man, weary from travel, meets the mender of roads. They address each other as "Jacques" to indicate their status as revolutionaries. The mender of roads directs the man to the chateau of the murdered Marquis. Later that night, the man sets the castle on fire. A rider from the chateau urges the village soldiers to help put out the fire and salvage the valuables there, but they refuse, and the villagers go inside their homes and put "candles in every dull little pane of glass." The peasants nearly kill Gabelle, the local tax collector, but he escapes to the roof of his house, where he watches the chateau burn. The narrator reports that scenes such as this are occurring all over France.

CHAPTER 24: DRAWN TO THE LOADSTONE ROCK
Three years pass. Political turmoil continues in France, causing England to become a refuge for persecuted aristocrats. Tellson's Bank in London becomes a "great gathering-place of Monseigneur." Tellson's has decided to dispatch Mr. Lorry to its Paris branch, in hopes that he can protect their valuable ledgers, papers, and records from destruction. Darnay arrives to persuade Lorry not to go, but Lorry insists, saying that he will bring Jerry Cruncher as his bodyguard.

Lorry receives an urgent letter, addressed to the Marquis St. Evrémonde, along with instructions for its delivery. Lorry laments the extreme difficulty of locating the Marquis, who has abandoned the estate willed to him by his murdered uncle. Darnay, careful to let no one suspect that he is in fact the missing Marquis, says that the Marquis is an acquaintance of his. He takes the letter, assuring Lorry that he will see it safely delivered. Darnay reads the letter, which contains a plea from Gabelle, whom the revolutionaries have imprisoned for his upkeep of the Marquis' property. Gabelle begs the new Marquis to return to France and save him. Darnay resolves

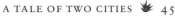

to go to Paris, with a "glorious vision of doing good." After writing a farewell letter to Lucie and Doctor Manette, he departs.

ANALYSIS

Before writing A *Tale of Two Cities,* Dickens had made one other attempt at historical fiction, entitled *Barnaby Rudge* (1841). Dissatisfied with the outcome of that venture, Dickens set out to craft a novel that combined the panorama of history with his typical cast of exaggerated characters. Critical opinion differs on whether he achieved a successful balance. Most critics agree that A *Tale of Two Cities* somewhat sacrifices its characters to its historical scope. They claim that the story lacks the memorable types of characters that vitalize Dickens's most popular novels, such as *The Old Curiosity Shop* and *David Copperfield.* However, debate continues as to whether Dickens's use of history ultimately warranted this sacrifice. Some consider the author's treatment of the revolution to be a triumphant success, while others believe that Dickens's indomitably fantastical imagination only waters down his history. Without doubt, Dickens relied heavily upon Thomas Carlyle's history of the French Revolution, a work that impressed Dickens greatly. Many of his details come directly from Carlyle's work, such as the description of the death of Foulon, which A *Tale of Two Cities* portrays as follows:

> *Once, he went aloft, and the rope broke, and they caught him shrieking . . . then, the rope was merciful, and held him, and his head was soon upon a pike, with grass enough in the mouth for all Saint Antoine to dance at the sight of.*

The similarity to Carlyle's portrayal of the same incident in *The French Revolution* is obvious:

> *Only with the third rope (for two ropes broke, and the quavering voice still pleaded) can he be so much as got hanged! His Body is dragged through the streets; his Head goes aloft on a pike, the mouth filled with grass: amid sounds as of Tophet, from a grass-eating people.*

Dickens acknowledges his debt to Carlyle in A *Tale of Two Cities'* preface, in which he states that he "hopes to add something to the popular and picturesque means of understanding [the French Revolution], though no one can hope to add anything to the philosophy of Mr Carlyle's wonderful book." Dickens's debt to Carlyle, however, runs deeper than the level of historical detail, extending to the book's philosophical outlook as well. Dickens believed, as Carlyle did, that history is an evolutionary phenomenon. In other words, one era must be destroyed before a new one can develop and thrive, or, as Carlyle noted, "each new age [is] born like the phoenix out of the ashes of the past."

Yet although Dickens promotes this view of history in which the destruction of the old makes way for the new, he remains ambivalent about the violence accompanying the cycles of eradication. While he acknowledges the evils and oppression that motivated the peasant uprising—he does this most notably in the chapters chronicling the events that lead up to the death of the Marquis—he never goes so far as to romanticize the revolutionaries' struggles or idealize their cause. Indeed, it is with great horror that he recounts the fall of the Bastille and the ensuing chaos in the streets. The violence may serve to cleanse society of the injustices of the French aristocracy, but it nevertheless creates its own sort of pollution. In describing the peasants' carefree return to eating, playing, and loving after their bloodthirsty execution of Foulon in Chapter 22, Dickens points toward a fundamentally corrupt side of the human soul.

Book the Third: The Track of a Storm
Chapters 1–5

Summary: Chapter 1: In Secret

Travel through France proves difficult for Darnay. Hostile revolutionaries frequently stop him and question him. Upon his arrival in Paris, the revolutionaries confine him to a prison called La Force. Darnay protests and reminds his jailers of his rights. However, the guard responds that, as an emigrant, Darnay—whom he refers to as Evrémonde—has no rights. The guard hands Darnay over to Defarge with the instructions, "In secret." As he is being led away, Darnay converses with the wine merchant. Defarge wonders aloud why Darnay would choose to return to France in the age of "that sharp female newly-born . . . called La Guillotine." Darnay asks Defarge for help, but Defarge refuses. At La Force, Darnay feels he has entered the world of the dead. A fellow prisoner welcomes him to the prison and says that he hopes that Darnay will not be kept "in secret"—the Anglicized form of *en secret*, meaning solitary confinement. But Darnay has indeed been sentenced to total isolation, and he soon finds himself in a cell measuring "five paces by four and a half."

SUMMARY: CHAPTER 2: THE GRINDSTONE

Lucie and Doctor Manette storm into the Paris branch of Tellson's Bank to find Mr. Lorry. They inform him that Darnay sits imprisoned in La Force. Manette remains confident that he can use his standing as a one-time prisoner of the Bastille to help rescue his son-in-law. Lorry sends Lucie into the back room of the bank so that he can speak to Manette in private. He and Manette look out into the courtyard, where throngs of people sharpen their weapons on a grindstone. Lorry explains that the mob is preparing to kill the prisoners. Manette rushes into the crowd, and soon a cry arises: "Help for the Bastille prisoner's kindred in La Force!"

SUMMARY: CHAPTER 3: THE SHADOW

Fearing that Lucie and Manette's presence might compromise the bank's business, Lorry ushers Lucie, her daughter, and Miss Pross to a nearby lodging. He leaves Jerry Cruncher to guard them. Back at Tellson's, Defarge approaches Lorry with a message from Manette. Following Manette's instructions, Lorry leads Defarge to Lucie. Defarge claims that Madame Defarge must accompany them, as she will familiarize herself with the faces of Lucie, her daughter, and Miss Pross, in order to better protect them in the future. The woman known as The Vengeance also comes. Upon arriving at the lodging, Defarge gives Lucie a note from the imprisoned Darnay. It urges her to take courage. Turning to Madame Defarge, Lucie begs her to show Darnay some mercy, but Madame Defarge coldly responds that the revolution will not stop for the sake of Lucie or her family.

SUMMARY: CHAPTER 4: CALM IN STORM

Four days later, Manette returns from La Force. Lorry notes a change in the once-fragile Manette, who now seems full of strength and power. Manette tells him that he has persuaded the Tribunal, a self-appointed body that tries and sentences the revolution's prisoners, to keep Darnay alive. Moreover, he has secured a job as the inspecting physician of three prisons, one of which is La Force. These duties will enable him to ensure Darnay's safety. Time passes, and France rages as though in a fever. The revolutionaries behead the king and queen, and the guillotine becomes a fixture in the Paris streets. Darnay remains in prison for a year and three months.

SUMMARY; CHAPTER 5: THE WOOD-SAWYER

While the family waits for Darnay's trial, Manette tells Lucie of a window in the prison from which Darnay might see her in the street. For two hours every day, Lucie stands in the area visible from this window. A wood-sawyer who works nearby talks with Lucie while she waits, pretending that his saw is a guillotine (it bears the inscription "Little Sainte Guillotine") and that each piece of wood that he cuts is the head of a prisoner. One day, a throng of people comes down the street, dancing a horrible and violent dance known as the Carmagnole. The dancers depart, and the distressed Lucie now sees her father standing before her. As he comforts Lucie, Madame Defarge happens by. She and Manette exchange salutes. Manette then tells Lucie that Darnay will stand trial on the following day and assures her that her husband will fare well in it.

ANALYSIS: CHAPTERS 1–5

The scene at the grindstone powerfully evokes the frantic and mindlessly violent mob of the revolution. A master of imagery, Dickens often connects one scene to another in such a manner that the images flow throughout the entire novel rather than stand in isolation. The reader feels this continuity as the crowd gathers around the grindstone to sharpen their weapons. The description of the people in blood-stained rags, "[not one] creature in the group free from the smear of blood," immediately recalls the breaking of the wine-cask outside Defarge's shop in Chapter 5; there, too, the people's rags are stained and "those who had been greedy with the staves of the cask, had acquired a tigerish smear about the mouth." These parallel scenes do more than testify to Dickens's artistry. They serve to place disparate motifs into symbolic relation. In repeating the motif of the red-stained peasants' rags, Dickens links wine with blood, invoking the Christian association between communion wine and the blood of Christ. However, Dickens complicates the symbol in his text. While the blood of Christ traditionally signifies salvation— Christians believe that Christ sacrificed his life for human deliverance from sin—Dickens's grisly depictions of the vicious, vengeful, and often sadistic revolutionaries express a deep skepticism in the redemptive power of political bloodshed.

Shadows constitute another symbol that permeates the entire novel, here providing the subheading for Chapter 3. Dickens uses light and dark much as a painter might, infusing his composition with a wide range of tone and depth. The reader can observe

Dickens's use of light and shadow at various instances in the novel. Notably, the chilling opening of the novel, in which the mail coach weaves its way through the darkness and fog, sets a tone of ominous mystery for the story; conversely, the sweet sunrise that opens Book the Second, Chapter 18, lends Lucie's wedding day an air of promise and happiness. In the current section, Madame Defarge casts a menacing shadow:

> The shadow attendant on Madame Defarge and her party seemed to fall so threatening and dark on the child, that her mother instinctively kneeled on the ground beside her, and held her to her breast. The shadow attendant on Madame Defarge and her party seemed then to fall, threatening and dark, on both the mother and the child.

The narrator's focus on the looming presence of Madame Defarge and on Lucie's inability to escape this woman's shadow establishes a tension between the gentle and nurturing Lucie—the "golden-haired doll"—and the dark and cold Madame Defarge, an unrelenting instrument of the revolution. Indeed, the narrator implicitly likens Madame Defarge's shadow, which "fall[s] . . . threatening and dark," to the guillotine blade that she is so eager to see making its fatal descent.

In Chapter 5, Dickens furthers this tension between Lucie's sweet goodness and the perverse malevolence of the revolution. The wood-sawyer who talks with Lucie in Chapter 5 possesses a grotesque zeal for decapitation, as evidenced by the religious nature of the moniker that he gives to his saw. He labels his imagined guillotine "Sainte"—that is, holy—illustrating his belief that the guillotine, in lopping off the heads of the aristocracy, is carrying out divine will. Similarly devoted but of opposite sympathy, Lucie waits steadfastly outside of her husband's prison, merely on the off-chance that Darnay might catch a glimpse of her. Whereas the violent and rambunctious Carmagnole dance, in which the wood-sawyer participates, symbolizes the ruthlessness of the revolution, the white snow that falls "quietly and . . . soft" in the very same chapter symbolizes Lucie's gentle soul and pure love for Darnay. When Madame Defarge passes by "like a shadow over the white road," the reader again senses the threat she poses to Lucie's happiness.

Book the Third: The Track of a Storm
Chapters 6–10

SUMMARY & ANALYSIS

Summary: Chapter 6: Triumph
A motley and bloodthirsty crowd assembles at the trial of Charles Darnay. When Doctor Manette is announced as Darnay's father-in-law, a happy cry goes up among the audience. The court hears testimony from Darnay, Manette, and Gabelle, establishing that Darnay long ago had renounced his title out of disapproval of the aristocracy's treatment of peasants. These factors, in addition to Darnay's status as the son-in-law of the much-loved martyr Manette, persuade the jury to acquit him. The crowd carries Darnay home in a chair on their shoulders.

Summary: Chapter 7: A Knock at the Door
The next day, although Manette rejoices in having saved Darnay's life, Lucie remains terrified for her husband. Later that afternoon, she reports hearing footsteps on the stairs, and soon a knock comes at the door. Four soldiers enter and re-arrest Darnay. Manette protests, but one of the soldiers reminds him that if the Republic demands a sacrifice from him, he must make that sacrifice. Manette asks one of the soldiers to give the name of Darnay's accuser. Though it is against the law to divulge such information, the soldier replies that he is carrying out the arrest according to statements made by Defarge, Madame Defarge, and one other individual. When Manette asks for the identity of this third person, the soldier replies that Manette will receive his answer the next day.

Summary: Chapter 8: A Hand at Cards
Meanwhile, Jerry Cruncher and Miss Pross discover Miss Pross's long-lost brother, Solomon, in a wine shop. Solomon scolds his sister for making a scene over their reunion. He cannot afford to be identified because he is working as a spy for the Republic. Meanwhile, Cruncher recognizes Solomon as the witness who accused Darnay of treason during his trial in England thirteen years earlier. He struggles to remember the man's name until Sydney Carton, who suddenly appears behind them, provides it: Barsad. Carton states that he has been in Paris for a day and has been lying low until he could be useful. He threatens to reveal Barsad's true identity to the revolutionaries unless the spy accompanies him to Tellson's.

Upon arriving at Tellson's, Carton informs Mr. Lorry and Jerry Cruncher that Darnay has been arrested again; he overheard Barsad discussing the news in a bar. Carton has a plan to help Darnay, should he be convicted, and he threatens to expose Barsad as an English spy should Barsad fail to cooperate. Carton reveals that he has seen Barsad conversing with Roger Cly, a known English spy. When Barsad counters that Cly is dead and presents the certificate of burial, Cruncher disproves the story by asserting that Cly's coffin contained only stones and dirt. Though Cruncher is unwilling to explain how he knows these details, Carton takes him at his word and again threatens to expose Barsad as an enemy of the Republic. Barsad finally gives in and agrees to help Carton with his secret plan.

SUMMARY: CHAPTER 9: THE GAME MADE

Lorry scolds Cruncher for leading a secret life (grave-robbing) outside his job at Tellson's. Cruncher hints that there may be many doctors involved in grave-robbing who bank at Tellson's. Cruncher then makes amends, saying that if Lorry will let young Jerry Cruncher inherit his own duties at the bank, he himself will become a gravedigger to make up for all the graves that he has "un-dug." After Barsad leaves, Carton tells Lorry and Cruncher that he has arranged a time to visit Darnay before his imminent execution. Carton reflects that a human being who has not secured the love of another has wasted his life, and Lorry agrees.

That night, as he wanders the streets of Paris, Carton thinks of Lucie. He enters a chemist's shop and buys a mysterious substance. The words spoken by the priest at his father's funeral echo through his mind: "I am the resurrection and the life, saith the Lord: he that believeth in me, though he were dead, yet shall he live: and whosoever liveth and believeth in me, shall never die." Carton helps a small girl across the muddy street, and she gives him a kiss. The priest's words echo again in his mind. He wanders until sunrise, then makes his way to the courthouse for Darnay's trial. The judge names Darnay's accusers: the Defarges and Doctor Manette. Manette reacts with shock and denies having ever denounced Darnay. Defarge then takes the stand and speaks of a letter that he found, hidden in 105 North Tower of the Bastille.

SUMMARY: CHAPTER 10: THE SUBSTANCE OF THE SHADOW

Defarge claims that Manette wrote the letter while imprisoned in the Bastille, and he reads it aloud. It tells the story of Manette's imprisonment. In 1757, a pair of brothers, one the Marquis Evrémonde (Darnay's father) and the other the next in line to be Marquis (Darnay's uncle, the man who ran over the child with his carriage in Book the Second, Chapter 7), ordered Doctor Manette to care for a young peasant woman, who was dying of a fever, and her brother, who was dying of a stab wound. The Marquis' brother had raped the young woman, killed her husband, and stabbed her brother, who died quickly. Although the woman was still alive, Manette failed to save her life. The next day a kind woman—the Marquis' wife and Darnay's mother—came to Manette's door. Having heard about the horrible things done to the peasant girl and her family, she offers to help the girl's sister, who was hidden away so the Marquis could not find her. Unfortunately, Manette does not know the sister's whereabouts. The next day, Manette was taken away and imprisoned in the Bastille on the orders of the Marquis Evrémonde. After hearing this story, the jury sentences Darnay to death, to pay for the sins of his father and uncle.

ANALYSIS: CHAPTERS 6–10

The echoing footsteps that Lucie hears in Chapter 21 of Book the Second now manifest themselves again, but this time they signify the immediate presence of pressing danger. No longer distant, dim, or scarcely audible, the footfalls in Chapter 7 announce the four soldiers come to take Darnay back to prison. Whereas the revolution only vaguely stirs Lucie when she sits in her comfortable parlor in England, it encroaches, physically and emotionally, upon her most intimate relationships now that she has come to Paris. This transformation of the revolution from an abstract notion into a direct presence in the lives of Lucie and Manette finds a parallel in the soldiers' words to them. In answering Manette's question as to the identity of Darnay's accusers, the soldiers first tell him that they are acting on the orders of Saint Antoine, the personified suburb of Paris at the heart of the revolution. However, Manette soon learns that Defarge and his wife have in fact occasioned the arrest. With the news of this betrayal by his former allies, the revolution reaches new heights of personal significance for Manette.

As the novel approaches its close, the reader encounters an ever-increasing number of coincidences, such as Miss Pross's discovery of her long-lost brother; Carton's timely arrival in the wine shop to identify Barsad; and Defarge's discovery of Manette's letter denouncing the Evrémonde family. Moments such as these, endemic to Victorian fiction, constitute a device called *deus ex machina* (literally: "god out of the machine"), a term that refers to improbable contrivances used by the author to resolve the plot. Modern readers, more accustomed to realistic narratives, usually consider such unlikely developments to reflect a weakness in the plot's conception. Even in Dickens's time, certain readers objected to the contrived feeling created by these coincidences. Wilkie Collins, for instance—the author of *The Frozen Deep,* the play that inspired *A Tale of Two Cities*—found the discovery of Manette's letter in Dickens's work highly unlikely. But defenders of this style of writing believe that Dickens conceived a world in which everything is so interconnected to everything else that coincidence—no matter how unlikely—is inevitable. Dickens's biographer, John Forster, defended the author thus:

> On the coincidences, resemblances, and surprises of
> life, Dickens liked especially to dwell, and few things
> moved his fancy so pleasantly. The world, he would say,
> was so much smaller than we thought it; we were all so
> connected by fate without knowing it; people supposed to
> be far apart were so constantly elbowing each other; and
> to-morrow bore so close a resemblance to nothing half so
> much as to yesterday.

The coincidences Dickens presents may seem excessive in number, but many critics have come to see these plot devices as yet another example of Dickens's talent for exaggeration. Just as his many caricatured figures serve to emphasize and comment on real human foibles, his coincidences and sudden surprising connections serve merely to exaggerate the frequency of what Dickens believed to be very real phenomena in our own world.

Regardless of how one feels about Carton's sudden appearance, one must acknowledge the transformation of his character as one of the novel's foremost achievements. Indeed, Carton proves the most psychologically complex and emotionally rich character that *A Tale of Two Cities* has to offer. By the time of his appearance in Paris, he has shed the skin of "the jackal." No longer insolent, lazy, and directionless, he emerges determined to save Darnay's life for the sake of the woman that he himself loves. He now has a purpose, and a purpose that he cherishes. In Chapter 9, the reader witnesses him preparing to make the ultimate sacrifice as he recites a passage from the Book of John (11.25–26). In the Christian tradition, worshippers speak these lines at the opening of the Burial Service in the Book of Common Prayer. Carton's utterance of these words has a dual significance. First, his words confirm that he has made a conscious decision to give of himself for Lucie's sake. (The reader might argue that Carton already has sacrificed himself to Lucie's benefit. However, although Carton has saved Darnay once before, in Book the Second, Chapter 3, this first occasion—his observation of the physical likeness that he and Darnay share—seemed more serendipitous than an act of valor performed deliberately to help Lucie.) Second, Carton's recitation of the biblical passage speaks beyond his personal psychology to the fates of the other characters in the novel, promising a final and satisfying resurrection.

Book the Third: The Track of a Storm
Chapters 11–15

Summary: Chapter 11: Dusk

The courtroom crowd pours into the streets to celebrate Darnay's condemnation. John Barsad, charged with ushering Darnay back to his cell, lets Lucie embrace her husband one last time. Darnay insists that Doctor Manette not blame himself for the trial's outcome. Darnay is escorted back to his cell to await his execution the following morning, and Carton escorts the grieving Lucie to her apartment. Carton tells Manette to try his influence one last time with the prosecutors and then meet him at Tellson's, though Lorry feels certain that there is no hope for Darnay, and Carton echoes the sentiment.

Summary: Chapter 12: Darkness

Carton goes to Defarge's wine shop. The Defarges marvel at how much he physically resembles the condemned Darnay. Carton overhears Madame Defarge's plan to accuse Lucie and Manette of spying, and to accuse Lucie's daughter as well. Defarge himself finds this course unnecessary, but his wife reminds him of her grievance against the family Evrémonde: she is the surviving sister of the woman and man killed by the Marquis and his brother. She demands the extermination of their heirs. Carton pays for his wine and returns to Tellson's.

At midnight, Manette arrives home completely out of his mind. He looks about madly for his shoemaking bench. After calming Manette, Carton takes from the doctor's coat the papers that will allow Lucie, the doctor, and the child to leave the city. He gives the documents to Lorry. Then, Carton gives Lorry his own papers, refusing to explain why. Afraid that the papers may soon be recalled because Madame Defarge intends to denounce the entire family, Carton insists to Lorry that time is of the essence: the family must leave tomorrow. Alone in the street that night, Carton utters a final good-bye and blessing to Lucie.

SUMMARY: CHAPTER 13: FIFTY-TWO

Fifty-two people have been condemned to die the next day. Darnay resolves to meet his death bravely. Carton appears at the door to Darnay's cell, and Darnay observes something new and bright in Carton's face. Carton tricks Darnay into switching clothes with him, dictates a letter of explanation, and then drugs him with the substance that he had purchased at the chemist's shop. He orders Barsad to carry the unconscious Darnay to the carriage waiting outside Tellson's. At two o'clock, guards take Carton from Darnay's cell, believing him to be Darnay. He stands in the long line of the condemned. A poor seamstress, also falsely sentenced to death, realizes that Carton is not Darnay and asks, "Are you dying for him?" He replies, "And his wife and child." Meanwhile, Barsad delivers the real Darnay to Manette, Lorry, and Lucie, and sends the carriage on its way. Lorry presents the family's papers at the city gates as they leave. They flee through the countryside, fearing pursuit.

SUMMARY: CHAPTER 14: THE KNITTING DONE

Meanwhile, Madame Defarge heads toward Lucie's apartment to try to catch Lucie in the illegal act of mourning a prisoner. Evidence of such a crime, she believes, will strengthen her case against the family. At the apartment, Miss Pross and Jerry Cruncher are in the middle of making final arrangements to depart Paris. To avoid drawing the suspicion that leaving together might engender, Miss Pross tells Cruncher to wait for her with the carriage at the cathedral. When Cruncher leaves, Madame Defarge barges in and demands to know Lucie's whereabouts. The women fight, and Madame Defarge draws a gun. In the struggle, however, Miss Pross shoots her. She meets Cruncher as planned and reports that she has gone deaf from the gunshot.

SUMMARY: CHAPTER 15: THE FOOTSTEPS DIE OUT FOREVER

> *Crush humanity out of shape once more . . . and it will*
> *twist itself into the same tortured forms. Sow the same*
> *seed of . . . oppression over again, and it will surely*
> *yield the same fruit according to its kind.*
>
> (See QUOTATIONS, *p. 62*)

Carton and the young seamstress reach the guillotine. The Vengeance and the other revolutionary women worry that Madame
Defarge will miss the beheading of Charles Darnay. The seamstress
reflects that the new Republic may make life easier for poor people
like herself and her surviving cousin. She kisses Carton and goes
calmly to her death. Carton then goes to his.

The narrator recounts that those who saw Carton die witnessed
a peaceful and even prophetic look on his face, and speculates confidently about Carton's final thoughts: Carton notes the fact that
the oppressors in the crowd "have risen on the destruction of the
old," but also realizes that, someday, Paris will recover from these
horrors and become beautiful. Also in these imagined last moments,
Carton sees Lucie and Darnay with a child named after himself. He
sees Manette happy and healthy and sees Lorry living a long and
peaceful life. He sees a future in which he holds a special place in
their hearts and in the hearts of generations hence. He sees his own
name "made illustrious," and the blots that he threw upon his life
fade away. According to the narrator, Carton dies in the knowledge
that "It is a far, far better thing that I do, than I have ever done; it is
a far, far better rest that I go to than I have ever known."

> *I see a beautiful city and a brilliant people rising from*
> *this abyss, and, in their struggles to be truly free, . . . I*
> *see the evil of this time . . . gradually making expiation*
> *for itself and wearing out.*
>
> (See QUOTATIONS, *p. 63*)

ANALYSIS: CHAPTERS 11–15

Dickens uses the figure of Miss Pross to emphasize the power of
love. As the devoted servant battles with Madame Defarge, he notes
that "the vigorous tenacity of love [is] always so much stronger
than hate." The showdown between the two women serves also
as a commentary on social order and revolution. Revolution, as
embodied by Madame Defarge, may prove fiercer and wilder, but

the social order that Miss Pross represents emerges as stronger and steadier. Although Dickens denounces the cruelty and vengefulness of Madame Defarge, he acknowledges the unavoidable fact of such people's existence in the world:

> And yet there is not in France, with its rich variety of soil and climate, a blade, a leaf, a root, a sprig, a peppercorn, which will grow to maturity under conditions more certain than those that have produced this horror. Crush humanity out of shape once more, under similar hammers, and it will twist itself into the same tortured forms. Sow the same seed of rapacious license and oppression over again, and it will surely yield the same fruit according to its kind.

Yet in noting the prevalence of evil, Dickens also shows an understanding of the processes by which evil arises. Madame Defarge certainly possesses a criminal bloodlust, but Dickens suggests her own tragic past and suffering, rather than any innate ill-will toward humanity, have transformed her into the despicable creature that she has become. As such, Dickens is not so interested in criticizing Madame Defarge specifically as he is in using her as an example of the vices that society perpetrates. Although, at the end of the novel, the narrator, using Carton's voice, prophesies a restored and replenished France—true to Carlyle's theory of history in which one era emerges "like a phoenix" out of the ashes of another—*A Tale of Two Cities* ultimately extends a cautionary word toward its readers. In certain sublime instances—such as Carton's self-sacrifice—death may beget life, but oppression can beget nothing other than itself.

The novel ends with something of a Christian paradox: life is achieved through death. Carton's sacrifice of his life enables him to live in a way that he otherwise could not, for this sacrifice—the only means by which Darnay can be saved—assures Carton a place in the hearts of others and allows him to have undertaken one truly meaningful and valuable act before dying. The final passage, in which the narrator imagines and records Carton's last thoughts, extends Carton's life beyond the moment of his death. He will live on in Lucie and Darnay, who will feel as deeply connected to him as they do to each other. He will live on in their child, who will bear his name and ambitiously follow a path that might have been Carton's own. Generations to come will honor his memory, endowing him with a glory that he could never have enjoyed had he continued living as Stryver's disaffected and drunken assistant. Carton's death emphasizes one of the novel's simpler philosophies—that love conquers all. Carton's love for Lucie allows him to overcome not only the purposelessness of his life but also his own death. Moreover, the event constitutes a Victorian ending, in that it provides the perfect resolution to various characters' problems. It ensures the continued happiness of Darnay and Lucie and it represents the redemption of the once spiritually aimless Carton.

The closing shift from third-person narration to the first-person supposed thoughts of Sydney Carton creates a powerful effect—it is as if Carton's beautiful act transcends even the narrator's control over the story. Indeed, the stunningly philosophical words that the narrator ascribes to Carton mirror Carton's quasi-religious ascension into the realm of the sublime. In his repetition of the phrase "I see" over the second to last four paragraphs, Dickens uses anaphora, a rhetorical device in which a phrase recurs at the beginning of successive clauses. These paragraphs then culminate in the spiritually edifying and uplifting anaphora of "It is a far, far better thing" and "It is a far, far better rest." This device lends the closing passages a soothing, peaceful tone, and, in its repetition, evokes the language of prayer and reverence. The harmony between the style and content of these final paragraphs leaves the reader with a feeling of complete resolution.

Important Quotations
Explained

1.   It was the best of times, it was the worst of times, it was
     the age of wisdom, it was the age of foolishness, it was
     the epoch of belief, it was the epoch of incredulity, it was
     the season of Light, it was the season of Darkness, it was
     the spring of hope, it was the winter of despair, we had
     everything before us, we had nothing before us, we were all
     going direct to Heaven, we were all going direct the other
     way. . . .

These famous lines, which open *A Tale of Two Cities,* hint at the
novel's central tension between love and family, on the one hand,
and oppression and hatred, on the other. The passage makes
marked use of anaphora, the repetition of a phrase at the beginning
of consecutive clauses—for example, "it was the age . . . it was the
age" and "it was the epoch . . . it was the epoch. . . ." This technique, along with the passage's steady rhythm, suggests that good
and evil, wisdom and folly, and light and darkness stand equally
matched in their struggle. The opposing pairs in this passage also
initiate one of the novel's most prominent motifs and structural figures—that of doubles, including London and Paris, Sydney Carton
and Charles Darnay, Miss Pross and Madame Defarge, and Lucie
and Madame Defarge.

2.   A wonderful fact to reflect upon, that every human
      creature is constituted to be that profound secret and
      mystery to every other. A solemn consideration, when I
      enter a great city by night, that every one of those darkly
      clustered houses encloses its own secret; that every room
      in every one of them encloses its own secret; that every
      beating heart in the hundreds of thousands of breasts
      there, is, in some of its imagin-ings, a secret to the heart
      nearest it! Something of the awfulness, even of Death itself,
      is referable to this.

The narrator makes this reflection at the beginning of Book the First,
Chapter 3, after Jerry Cruncher delivers a cryptic message to Jarvis
Lorry in the darkened mail coach. Lorry's mission—to recover the
long-imprisoned Doctor Manette and "recall" him to life—establishes the essential dilemma that he and other characters face: namely, that human beings constitute perpetual mysteries to one another
and always remain somewhat locked away, never fully reachable by
outside minds. This fundamental inscrutability proves most evident
in the case of Manette, whose private sufferings force him to relapse
throughout the novel into bouts of cobbling, an occupation that he
first took up in prison. Throughout the novel, Manette mentally
returns to his prison, bound more by his own recollections than by
any attempt of the other characters to "recall" him into the present. This passage's reference to death also evokes the deep secret
revealed in Carton's self-sacrifice at the end of the novel. The exact
profundity of his love and devotion for Lucie remains obscure until
he commits to dying for her; the selflessness of his death leaves the
reader to wonder at the ways in which he might have manifested this
great love in life.

3.   The wine was red wine, and had stained the ground of
     the narrow street in the suburb of Saint Antoine, in Paris,
     where it was spilled. It had stained many hands, too, and
     many faces, and many naked feet, and many wooden
     shoes. The hands of the man who sawed the wood, left red
     marks on the billets; and the forehead of the woman who
     nursed her baby, was stained with the stain of the old rag
     she wound about her head again. Those who had been
     greedy with the staves of the cask, had acquired a tigerish
     smear about the mouth; and one tall joker so besmirched,
     his head more out of a long squalid bag of a night-cap than
     in it, scrawled upon a wall with his finger dipped in muddy
     wine-lees—blood.

This passage, taken from Book the First, Chapter 5, describes the
scramble after a wine cask breaks outside Defarge's wine shop. This
episode opens the novel's examination of Paris and acts as a potent
depiction of the peasants' hunger. These oppressed individuals are
not only physically starved—and thus willing to slurp wine from
the city streets—but are also hungry for a new world order, for justice and freedom from misery. In this passage, Dickens foreshadows
the lengths to which the peasants' desperation will take them. This
scene is echoed later in the novel when the revolutionaries—now
similarly smeared with red, but the red of blood—gather around the
grindstone to sharpen their weapons. The emphasis here on the idea
of staining, as well as the scrawling of the word *blood*, furthers this
connection, as does the appearance of the wood-sawyer, who later
scares Lucie with his mock guillotine in Book the Third, Chapter
5. Additionally, the image of the wine lapping against naked feet
anticipates the final showdown between Miss Pross and Madame
Defarge in Book the Third, Chapter 14: "The basin fell to the ground
broken, and the water flowed to the feet of Madame Defarge. By
strange stern ways, and through much staining of blood, those feet
had come to meet that water."

QUOTATIONS

4.   Along the Paris streets, the death-carts rumble, hollow and
     harsh. Six tumbrels carry the day's wine to La Guillotine.
     All the devouring and insatiate Monsters imagined
     since imagination could record itself, are fused in one
     realization, Guillotine. And yet there is not in France, with
     its rich variety of soil and climate, a blade, a leaf, a root,
     a sprig, a peppercorn, which will grow to maturity under
     conditions more certain than those that have produced this
     horror. Crush humanity out of shape once more, under
     similar hammers, and it will twist itself into the same
     tortured forms. Sow the same seed of rapacious license
     and oppression over again, and it will surely yield the same
     fruit according to its kind.

In this concise and beautiful passage, which occurs in the final
chapter of the novel, Dickens summarizes his ambivalent attitude
toward the French Revolution. The author stops decidedly short
of justifying the violence that the peasants use to overturn the
social order, personifying "La Guillotine" as a sort of drunken
lord who consumes human lives—"the day's wine." Nevertheless,
Dickens shows a thorough understanding of how such violence
and bloodlust can come about. The cruel aristocracy's oppression of the poor "sow[s] the same seed of rapacious license" in
the poor and compels them to persecute the aristocracy and other
enemies of the revolution with equal brutality. Dickens perceives
these revolutionaries as "[c]rush[ed] . . . out of shape" and having
been "hammer[ed] . . . into . . . tortured forms." These depictions
evidence his belief that the lower classes' fundamental goodness
has been perverted by the terrible conditions under which the aristocracy has forced them to live.

QUOTATIONS

5.   I see a beautiful city and a brilliant people rising from
     this abyss, and, in their struggles to be truly free, in their
     triumphs and defeats, through long years to come, I see the
     evil of this time and of the previous time of which this is
     the natural birth, gradually making expiation for itself and
     wearing out. . . .
         I see that child who lay upon her bosom and who bore
     my name, a man winning his way up in that path of life
     which once was mine. I see him winning it so well, that my
     name is made illustrious there by the light of his. . . .
         It is a far, far better thing that I do, than I have ever
     done; it is a far, far better rest I go to than I have ever
     known.

Though much debate has arisen regarding the value and meaning
of Sydney Carton's sacrifice at the end of the novel, the surest key to
interpretation rests in the thoughts contained in this passage, which
the narrator attributes to Carton as he awaits his sacrificial death.
This passage, which occurs in the final chapter, prophesies two res-
urrections: one personal, the other national. In a novel that seeks
to examine the nature of revolution—the overturning of one way
of life for another—the struggles of France and of Sydney Carton
mirror each other. Here, Dickens articulates the outcome of those
struggles: just as Paris will "ris[e] from [the] abyss" of the French
Revolution's chaotic and bloody violence, so too will Carton be
reborn into glory after a virtually wasted life. In the prophecy that
Paris will become "a beautiful city" and that Carton's name will be
"made illustrious," the reader sees evidence of Dickens's faith in the
essential goodness of humankind. The very last thoughts attributed
to Carton, in their poetic use of repetition, register this faith as a
calm and soothing certainty.

QUOTATIONS

Key Facts

FULL TITLE
  A Tale of Two Cities

AUTHOR
  Charles Dickens

TYPE OF WORK
  Novel

GENRE
  Historical fiction

LANGUAGE
  English

TIME AND PLACE WRITTEN
  1859, London

DATE OF FIRST PUBLICATION
  Published in weekly serial form between April 20, 1859, and
  November 26, 1859

PUBLISHER
  Chapman and Hall

NARRATOR
  The narrator is anonymous and can be thought of as Dickens
  himself. The narrator maintains a clear sympathy for the story's
  morally good characters, including Sydney Carton, Charles
  Darnay, Doctor Manette, and Lucie Manette. Though he criticizes ruthless and hateful figures such as Madame Defarge,
  who cannot appreciate love, he understands that oppression
  has made these characters the bloodthirsty creatures they have
  become.

POINT OF VIEW
  The narrator speaks in the third person, deftly switching
  his focus between cities and among several characters. The
  narrator is also omniscient—not only revealing the thoughts,
  emotions, and motives of the characters, but also supplying

historical context to the events that occur, commenting confidently upon them.

TONE

Sentimental, sympathetic, sarcastic, horrified, grotesque, grim

TENSE

Past

SETTING (TIME)

1775–1793

SETTING (PLACE)

London and its outskirts; Paris and its outskirts

PROTAGONIST

Charles Darnay or Sydney Carton

MAJOR CONFLICT

Madame Defarge seeks revenge against Darnay for his relation to the odious Marquis Evrémonde; Carton, Manette, Lucie, and Jarvis Lorry strive to protect Darnay from the bloodthirsty revolutionaries' guillotine.

RISING ACTION

The ongoing murder of aristocrats after the storming of the Bastille; Darnay's decision to go to Paris to save Gabelle; the Defarges' demand that Darnay be arrested

CLIMAX

During a court trial, Defarge reads aloud a letter that he has discovered, which Manette wrote during his imprisonment in the Bastille and which indicts Darnay as a member of the cruel aristocratic lineage of Evrémonde (Book the Third, Chapter 10). In this climactic moment, it becomes clear that Madame Defarge's overzealous hatred of Darnay can end only in death—either his or hers.

FALLING ACTION

The jury's sentencing of Darnay to death; Darnay's wish that Manette not blame himself; Carton's decision to sacrifice his life to save Darnay

KEY FACTS

THEMES

The ever-present possibility of resurrection; the necessity of sacrifice; the tendency toward violence and oppression in revolutionaries

MOTIFS

Doubles; shadows and darkness; imprisonment

SYMBOLS

The wine that spills out of the cask in Book the First, Chapter 5, symbolizes the peasants' hunger and the blood that will be let when the revolution comes into full swing; Madame Defarge's knitting symbolizes the vengefulness of the common people; the Marquis is a symbol of pure evil—the Gorgon's head symbolizes his absolute coldness toward the suffering of the poor.

FORESHADOWING

The wine cask breaking outside Defarge's wine shop; the echoing footsteps in the Manettes' sitting room; the resemblance between Carton and Darnay; Carton's indication of this resemblance in a London court, which results in Darnay's acquittal; Doctor Manette's reaction after learning Darnay's true identity

STUDY QUESTIONS

1.   *Discuss at least one way in which Dickens parallels the
      personal and the political in* A TALE OF TWO CITIES.

In his dual focus on the French Revolution and the individual lives
of his characters, Dickens draws many comparisons between the
historical developments taking place and the characters' triumphs
and travails. Perhaps the most direct example of this parallel comes
in the final chapter of the novel, in which Dickens matches Sydney
Carton's death with the French Revolution's most frenzied violence,
linking the two through the concept of resurrection.

   Throughout the novel, Carton struggles to free himself from a
life of apathy and meaninglessness while the French lower classes
fight for political emancipation. Each of these struggles involves
death—Carton decides to give his life so that Charles Darnay may
escape, and the revolutionaries make a spectator sport out of the
execution of aristocrats. Still, each struggle holds the promise of
renewed life. Nowhere is this promise more evident than in the
prophecy that the narrator ascribes to Carton at the novel's end.
Here, Carton envisions a new city rising up from the ashes of
the ruined Paris as clearly as he sees Lucie, Darnay, and their son
celebrating and extending his life as a man of worth and honor.
Dickens thus closes his novel with a note of triumphant hope both
political and personal.

2.   *One of the novel's most important motifs is the figure
      of the double. What is the effect of Dickens's doubling
      technique? Does he use doubles to draw contrasts,
      comparisons, or both?*

From early on in the novel, various characters seemed paired as
opposites. Darnay, for instance, appears capable and accomplished,
while Carton seems lazy and lacks ambition. Similarly, Miss Pross
represents respectable English order while Madame Defarge embodies its opposite: hot-blooded revolution. As the novel progresses,
however, these doubled characters come to relate more as twins
than as opposites. Both Carton and Darnay share a common love

for Lucie, and Lucie exerts a power over Carton that enables him to shed his skin as a "jackal" and adopt a life that actually may exceed Darnay's in terms of devotion and heroism. A common ground exists even between Miss Pross and Madame Defarge. The two women share a sense of uncompromising duty, as becomes manifest in their confrontation in Lucie's apartment. Miss Pross proves as fiercely devoted to Lucie's life and safety as Madame Defarge is to the idea of a new French Republic purged of all aristocrats. Each is willing to give up her life for her beliefs. In revealing these resemblances, Dickens suggests that even seeming opposites can possess underlying similarities. This gesture, along with Dickens's inclusion of multiple coincidences in his plot, contributes to the author's larger message that human beings inhabit a world of multiple hidden patterns and connections.

3. *Discuss Dickens's use of foreshadowing in* A TALE OF TWO CITIES.

Dickens makes frequent use of foreshadowing, as it allows him to build suspense throughout his narrative and imbue it with a haunting atmosphere. He fills the novel with details that anticipate future events. For example, the wine cask breaking in the street and the echoing footsteps that can be heard in the Manettes' apartment hint to the reader about the imminence of the great and violent mob that eventually overtakes Paris. In this way, the reader becomes more aware of the situation than Dickens's characters and feels ever more emotionally and psychologically involved in the narrative. Given that Dickens published *A Tale of Two Cities* in short, weekly installments, this technique was a particularly effective means of sustaining the reader's interest in the novel. The reader was teased by hints of terrific events on the horizon and satisfied only by reading (and first buying) further installments.

How to Write Literary Analysis

The Literary Essay: A Step-by-Step Guide

When you read for pleasure, your only goal is enjoyment. You might find yourself reading to get caught up in an exciting story, to learn about an interesting time or place, or just to pass time. Maybe you're looking for inspiration, guidance, or a reflection of your own life. There are as many different, valid ways of reading a book as there are books in the world.

When you read a work of literature in an English class, however, you're being asked to read in a special way: you're being asked to perform *literary analysis*. To analyze something means to break it down into smaller parts and then examine how those parts work, both individually and together. Literary analysis involves examining all the parts of a novel, play, short story, or poem—elements such as character, setting, tone, and imagery—and thinking about how the author uses those elements to create certain effects.

A literary essay isn't a book review: you're not being asked whether or not you liked a book or whether you'd recommend it to another reader. A literary essay also isn't like the kind of book report you wrote when you were younger, where your teacher wanted you to summarize the book's action. A high school- or college-level literary essay asks, "How does this piece of literature actually work?" "How does it do what it does?" and, "Why might the author have made the choices he or she did?"

The Seven Steps
No one is born knowing how to analyze literature; it's a skill you learn and a process you can master. As you gain more practice with this kind of thinking and writing, you'll be able to craft a method that works best for you. But until then, here are seven basic steps to writing a well-constructed literary essay:

1. *Ask questions*
2. *Collect evidence*
3. *Construct a thesis*

4. Develop and organize arguments
5. Write the introduction
6. Write the body paragraphs
7. Write the conclusion

_____

1. ASK QUESTIONS

When you're assigned a literary essay in class, your teacher will often provide you with a list of writing prompts. Lucky you! Now all you have to do is choose one. Do yourself a favor and pick a topic that interests you. You'll have a much better (not to mention easier) time if you start off with something you enjoy thinking about. If you are asked to come up with a topic by yourself, though, you might start to feel a little panicked. Maybe you have too many ideas—or none at all. Don't worry. Take a deep breath and start by asking yourself these questions:

- **What struck you?** Did a particular image, line, or scene linger in your mind for a long time? If it fascinated you, chances are you can draw on it to write a fascinating essay.

- **What confused you?** Maybe you were surprised to see a character act in a certain way, or maybe you didn't understand why the book ended the way it did. Confusing moments in a work of literature are like a loose thread in a sweater: if you pull on it, you can unravel the entire thing. Ask yourself why the author chose to write about that character or scene the way he or she did and you might tap into some important insights about the work as a whole.

- **Did you notice any patterns?** Is there a phrase that the main character uses constantly or an image that repeats throughout the book? If you can figure out how that pattern weaves through the work and what the significance of that pattern is, you've almost got your entire essay mapped out.

- **Did you notice any contradictions or ironies?** Great works of literature are complex; great literary essays recognize and explain those complexities. Maybe the title (*Happy Days*) totally disagrees with the book's subject matter (hungry orphans dying in the woods). Maybe the main character acts one way around his family and a completely different way around his friends and associates. If you can find a way to explain a work's contradictory elements, you've got the seeds of a great essay.

At this point, you don't need to know exactly what you're going to say about your topic; you just need a place to begin your exploration. You can help direct your reading and brainstorming by formulating your topic as a *question,* which you'll then try to answer in your essay. The best questions invite critical debates and discussions, not just a rehashing of the summary. Remember, you're looking for something you can *prove or argue* based on evidence you find in the text. Finally, remember to keep the scope of your question in mind: is this a topic you can adequately address within the word or page limit you've been given? Conversely, is this a topic big enough to fill the required length?

GOOD QUESTIONS

> *"Are Romeo and Juliet's parents responsible for the deaths of their children?"*
>> *"Why do pigs keep showing up in* LORD OF THE FLIES*?"*
>> *"Are Dr. Frankenstein and his monster alike? How?"*

BAD QUESTIONS

> *"What happens to Scout in* TO KILL A MOCKINGBIRD*?"*
> *"What do the other characters in* JULIUS CAESAR *think about Caesar?"*
> *"How does Hester Prynne in* THE SCARLET LETTER *remind me of my sister?"*

---

2. COLLECT EVIDENCE

Once you know what question you want to answer, it's time to scour the book for things that will help you answer the question. Don't worry if you don't know what you want to say yet—right now you're just collecting ideas and material and letting it all percolate. Keep track of passages, symbols, images, or scenes that deal with your topic. Eventually, you'll start making connections between these examples and your thesis will emerge.

Here's a brief summary of the various parts that compose each and every work of literature. These are the elements that you will analyze in your essay, and which you will offer as evidence to support your arguments. For more on the parts of literary works, see the Glossary of Literary Terms at the end of this section.

LITERARY ANALYSIS

ELEMENTS OF STORY   These are the *what*s of the work—what happens, where it happens, and to whom it happens.

- **Plot:** All of the events and actions of the work.

- **Character:** The people who act and are acted upon in a literary work. The main character of a work is known as the *protagonist.*

- **Conflict:** The central tension in the work. In most cases, the protagonist wants something, while opposing forces (antagonists) hinder the protagonist's progress.

- **Setting:** When and where the work takes place. Elements of setting include location, time period, time of day, weather, social atmosphere, and economic conditions.

- **Narrator:** The person telling the story. The narrator may straightforwardly report what happens, convey the subjective opinions and perceptions of one or more characters, or provide commentary and opinion in his or her own voice.

- **Themes:** The main idea or message of the work—usually an abstract idea about people, society, or life in general. A work may have many themes, which may be in tension with one another.

ELEMENTS OF STYLE   These are the *how*s—how the characters speak, how the story is constructed, and how language is used throughout the work.

- **Structure and organization:** How the parts of the work are assembled. Some novels are narrated in a linear, chronological fashion, while others skip around in time. Some plays follow a traditional three- or five-act structure, while others are a series of loosely connected scenes. Some authors deliberately leave gaps in their works, leaving readers to puzzle out the missing information. A work's structure and organization can tell you a lot about the kind of message it wants to convey.

- **Point of view:** The perspective from which a story is told. In *first-person point of view,* the narrator involves him or herself in the story. ("I went to the store"; "We watched in horror as the bird slammed into the window.") A first-person narrator is usually the protagonist of the work, but not always. In *third-person point of view,* the narrator does not participate in the story. A third-person narrator may closely follow a specific character, recounting that individual character's thoughts or experiences, or it may be what we call an *omniscient* narrator. Omniscient narrators see and know all: they can witness any event in any time or place and are privy to the inner thoughts and feelings of all characters. Remember that the narrator and the author are not the same thing!

- **Diction:** Word choice. Whether a character uses dry, clinical language or flowery prose with lots of exclamation points can tell you a lot about his or her attitude and personality.

- **Syntax:** Word order and sentence construction. Syntax is a crucial part of establishing an author's narrative voice. Ernest Hemingway, for example, is known for writing in very short, straightforward sentences, while James Joyce characteristically wrote in long, incredibly complicated lines.

- **Tone:** The mood or feeling of the text. Diction and syntax often contribute to the tone of a work. A novel written in short, clipped sentences that use small, simple words might feel brusque, cold, or matter-of-fact.

- **Imagery:** Language that appeals to the senses, representing things that can be seen, smelled, heard, tasted, or touched.

- **Figurative language:** Language that is not meant to be interpreted literally. The most common types of figurative language are *metaphors* and *similes,* which compare two unlike things in order to suggest a similarity between them— for example, "All the world's a stage," or "The moon is like a ball of green cheese." (Metaphors say one thing *is* another thing; similes claim that one thing is *like* another thing.)

---

3. CONSTRUCT A THESIS

When you've examined all the evidence you've collected and know how you want to answer the question, it's time to write your thesis statement. A *thesis* is a claim about a work of literature that needs to be supported by evidence and arguments. The thesis statement is the heart of the literary essay, and the bulk of your paper will be spent trying to prove this claim. A good thesis will be:

- **Arguable.** "*The Great Gatsby* describes New York society in the 1920s" isn't a thesis—it's a fact.

LITERARY ANALYSIS

- **Provable through textual evidence**. "*Hamlet* is a confusing but ultimately very well-written play" is a weak thesis because it offers the writer's personal opinion about the book. Yes, it's arguable, but it's not a claim that can be proved or supported with examples taken from the play itself.

- **Surprising**. "Both George and Lenny change a great deal in *Of Mice and Men*" is a weak thesis because it's obvious. A really strong thesis will argue for a reading of the text that is not immediately apparent.

- **Specific**. "Dr. Frankenstein's monster tells us a lot about the human condition" is *almost* a really great thesis statement, but it's still too vague. What does the writer mean by "a lot"? *How* does the monster tell us so much about the human condition?

GOOD THESIS STATEMENTS

Question: In *Romeo and Juliet*, which is more powerful in shaping the lovers' story: fate or foolishness?

Thesis: "Though Shakespeare defines Romeo and Juliet as 'star-crossed lovers' and images of stars and planets appear throughout the play, a closer examination of that celestial imagery reveals that the stars are merely witnesses to the characters' foolish activities and not the causes themselves."

Question: How does the bell jar function as a symbol in Sylvia Plath's *The Bell Jar*?

Thesis: "A bell jar is a bell-shaped glass that has three basic uses: to hold a specimen for observation, to contain gases, and to maintain a vacuum. The bell jar appears in each of these capacities in *The Bell Jar*, Plath's semi-autobiographical novel, and each appearance marks a different stage in Esther's mental breakdown."

Question: Would Piggy in *The Lord of the Flies* make a good island leader if he were given the chance?

Thesis: "Though the intelligent, rational, and innovative Piggy has the mental characteristics of a good leader, he ultimately lacks the social skills necessary to be an effective one. Golding emphasizes this point by giving Piggy a foil in the charismatic Jack, whose magnetic personality allows him to capture and wield power effectively, if not always wisely."

4. DEVELOP AND ORGANIZE ARGUMENTS

The reasons and examples that support your thesis will form the middle paragraphs of your essay. Since you can't really write your thesis statement until you know how you'll structure your argument, you'll probably end up working on steps 3 and 4 at the same time.

There's no single method of argumentation that will work in every context. One essay prompt might ask you to compare and contrast two characters, while another asks you to trace an image through a given work of literature. These questions require different kinds of answers and therefore different kinds of arguments. Below, we'll discuss three common kinds of essay prompts and some strategies for constructing a solid, well-argued case.

TYPES OF LITERARY ESSAYS

- **Compare and contrast**

  Compare and contrast the characters of Huck and Jim in THE ADVENTURES OF HUCKLEBERRY FINN.

  Chances are you've written this kind of essay before. In an academic literary context, you'll organize your arguments the same way you would in any other class. You can either go *subject by subject* or *point by point*. In the former, you'll discuss one character first and then the second. In the latter, you'll choose several traits (attitude toward life, social status, images and metaphors associated with the character) and devote a paragraph to each. You may want to use a mix of these two approaches—for example, you may want to spend a paragraph a piece broadly sketching Huck's and Jim's personalities before transitioning into a paragraph or two that describes a few key points of comparison. This can be a highly effective strategy if you want to make a counterintuitive argument—that, despite seeming to be totally different, the two objects being compared are actually similar in a very important way (or vice versa). Remember that your essay should reveal something fresh or unexpected about the text, so think beyond the obvious parallels and differences.

- **Trace**

  Choose an image—for example, birds, knives, or eyes—and trace that image throughout MACBETH.

  Sounds pretty easy, right? All you need to do is read the play, underline every appearance of a knife in *Macbeth,* and then list them in your essay in the order they appear, right? Well, not exactly. Your teacher doesn't want a simple catalog of examples. He or she wants to see you make *connections* between those examples—that's the difference between summarizing and analyzing. In the *Macbeth* example above, think about the different contexts in which knives appear in the play and to what effect. In *Macbeth,* there are real knives and imagined knives; knives that kill and knives that simply threaten. Categorize and classify your examples to give them some order. Finally, always keep the overall effect in mind. After you choose and analyze your examples, you should come to some greater understanding about the work, as well as your chosen image, symbol, or phrase's role in developing the major themes and stylistic strategies of that work.

- **Debate**

   Is the society depicted in 1984 *good for its citizens?*

   In this kind of essay, you're being asked to debate a moral, ethical, or aesthetic issue regarding the work. You might be asked to judge a character or group of characters (*Is Caesar responsible for his own demise?*) or the work itself (*Is* JANE EYRE *a feminist novel?*). For this kind of essay, there are two important points to keep in mind. First, don't simply base your arguments on your personal feelings and reactions. Every literary essay expects you to read and analyze the work, so search for evidence in the text. What do characters in 1984 have to say about the government of Oceania? What images does Orwell use that might give you a hint about his attitude toward the government? As in any debate, you also need to make sure that you define all the necessary terms before you begin to argue your case. What does it mean to be a "good" society? What makes a novel "feminist"? You should define your terms right up front, in the first paragraph after your introduction.

   Second, remember that strong literary essays make contrary and surprising arguments. Try to think outside the box. In the 1984 example above, it seems like the obvious answer would be no, the totalitarian society depicted in Orwell's novel is *not* good for its citizens. But can you think of any arguments for the opposite side? Even if your final assertion is that the novel depicts a cruel, repressive, and therefore harmful society, acknowledging and responding to the counterargument will strengthen your overall case.

5. WRITE THE INTRODUCTION

Your introduction sets up the entire essay. It's where you present your topic and articulate the particular issues and questions you'll be addressing. It's also where you, as the writer, introduce yourself to your readers. A persuasive literary essay immediately establishes its writer as a knowledgeable, authoritative figure.

An introduction can vary in length depending on the overall length of the essay, but in a traditional five-paragraph essay it should be no longer than one paragraph. However long it is, your introduction needs to:

- **Provide any necessary context.** Your introduction should situate the reader and let him or her know what to expect. What book are you discussing? Which characters? What topic will you be addressing?

- **Answer the "So what?" question.** Why is this topic important, and why is your particular position on the topic noteworthy? Ideally, your introduction should pique the reader's interest by suggesting how your argument is surprising or otherwise counterintuitive. Literary essays make unexpected connections and reveal less-than-obvious truths.

- **Present your thesis.** This usually happens at or very near the end of your introduction.

- **Indicate the shape of the essay to come.** Your reader should finish reading your introduction with a good sense of the scope of your essay as well as the path you'll take toward proving your thesis. You don't need to spell out every step, but you do need to suggest the organizational pattern you'll be using.

Your introduction should not:

- **Be vague.** Beware of the two killer words in literary analysis: *interesting* and *important*. Of course the work, question, or example is interesting and important—that's why you're writing about it!

- **Open with any grandiose assertions.** Many student readers think that beginning their essays with a flamboyant statement such as, "Since the dawn of time, writers have been fascinated with the topic of free will," makes them sound important and commanding. You know what? It actually sounds pretty amateurish.

- **Wildly praise the work.** Another typical mistake student writers make is extolling the work or author. Your teacher doesn't need to be told that "Shakespeare is perhaps the greatest writer in the English language." You can mention a work's reputation in passing—by referring to *The Adventures of Huckleberry Finn* as "Mark Twain's enduring classic," for example—but don't make a point of bringing it up unless that reputation is key to your argument.

- **Go off-topic.** Keep your introduction streamlined and to the point. Don't feel the need to throw in all kinds of bells and whistles in order to impress your reader—just get to the point as quickly as you can, without skimping on any of the required steps.

---

6. WRITE THE BODY PARAGRAPHS

Once you've written your introduction, you'll take the arguments you developed in step 4 and turn them into your body paragraphs. The organization of this middle section of your essay will largely be determined by the argumentative strategy you use, but no matter how you arrange your thoughts, your body paragraphs need to do the following:

- **Begin with a strong topic sentence.** Topic sentences are like signs on a highway: they tell the reader where they are and where they're going. A good topic sentence not only alerts readers to what issue will be discussed in the following paragraph but also gives them a sense of what argument will be made *about* that issue. "Rumor and gossip play an important role in *The Crucible*" isn't a strong topic sentence because it doesn't tell us very much. "The community's constant gossiping creates an environment that allows false accusations to flourish" is a much stronger topic sentence—it not only tells us *what* the paragraph will discuss (gossip) but *how* the paragraph will discuss the topic (by showing how gossip creates a set of conditions that leads to the play's climactic action).

- **Fully and completely develop a single thought.** Don't skip around in your paragraph or try to stuff in too much material. Body paragraphs are like bricks: each individual

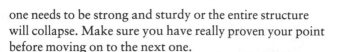

one needs to be strong and sturdy or the entire structure will collapse. Make sure you have really proven your point before moving on to the next one.

- **Use transitions effectively.** Good literary essay writers know that each paragraph must be clearly and strongly linked to the material around it. Think of each paragraph as a response to the one that precedes it. Use transition words and phrases such as *however, similarly, on the contrary, therefore,* and *furthermore* to indicate what kind of response you're making.

---

7. Write the Conclusion

Just as you used the introduction to ground your readers in the topic before providing your thesis, you'll use the conclusion to quickly summarize the specifics learned thus far and then hint at the broader implications of your topic. A good conclusion will:

- **Do more than simply restate the thesis.** If your thesis argued that *The Catcher in the Rye* can be read as a Christian allegory, don't simply end your essay by saying, "And that is why *The Catcher in the Rye* can be read as a Christian allegory." If you've constructed your arguments well, this kind of statement will just be redundant.

- **Synthesize the arguments, not summarize them.** Similarly, don't repeat the details of your body paragraphs in your conclusion. The reader has already read your essay, and chances are it's not so long that they've forgotten all your points by now.

- **Revisit the "So what?" question.** In your introduction, you made a case for why your topic and position are important. You should close your essay with the same sort of gesture. What do your readers know now that they didn't know before? How will that knowledge help them better appreciate or understand the work overall?

- **Move from the specific to the general.** Your essay has most likely treated a very specific element of the work—a single character, a small set of images, or a particular passage. In your conclusion, try to show how this narrow discussion has wider implications for the work overall. If your essay on *To Kill a Mockingbird* focused on the character of Boo Radley, for example, you might want to include a bit in your conclusion about how he fits into the novel's larger message about childhood, innocence, or family life.

- **Stay relevant.** Your conclusion should suggest new directions of thought, but it shouldn't be treated as an opportunity to pad your essay with all the extra, interesting ideas you came up with during your brainstorming sessions but couldn't fit into the essay proper. Don't attempt to stuff in unrelated queries or too many abstract thoughts.

- **Avoid making overblown closing statements.** A conclusion should open up your highly specific, focused discussion, but it should do so without drawing a sweeping lesson about life or human nature. Making such observations may be part of the point of reading, but it's almost always a mistake in essays, where these observations tend to sound overly dramatic or simply silly.

A+ Essay Checklist

Congratulations! If you've followed all the steps we've outlined above, you should have a solid literary essay to show for all your efforts. What if you've got your sights set on an A+? To write the kind of superlative essay that will be rewarded with a perfect grade, keep the following rubric in mind. These are the qualities that teachers expect to see in a truly A+ essay. How does yours stack up?

- ✓ Demonstrates a thorough understanding of the book
- ✓ Presents an original, compelling argument
- ✓ Thoughtfully analyzes the text's formal elements
- ✓ Uses appropriate and insightful examples
- ✓ Structures ideas in a logical and progressive order
- ✓ Demonstrates a mastery of sentence construction, transitions, grammar, spelling, and word choice

LITERARY ANALYSIS

SUGGESTED ESSAY TOPICS

1. *Some critics charge that Dickens, in much of his work, failed to create meaningful characters because he exaggerated them to parodic extremes. Do you find this a fair assessment of his characterization in* A TALE OF TWO CITIES? *Does the author's use of caricature detract from his novel's ability to speak to human nature?*

2. *Dickens relies heavily on coincidence to fuel the plot of* A TALE OF TWO CITIES: *letters are found bearing crucial information, for example, and long-lost brothers are discovered in crowded public places. Do such incidents strengthen or weaken the plot and overall themes of the novel?*

3. *Discuss Dickens's attitude toward the French Revolution. Does he sympathize with the revolutionaries?*

4. *Based on Dickens's portrayals of the villainous characters in his novel (particularly Madame Defarge), what conclusions might the reader draw about the author's notions of human evil? Does he seem to think that people are born evil? If so, do they lack the ability to change? Or does he suggest that circumstances drive human beings to their acts of cruelty?*

A+ STUDENT ESSAY

> Analyze Dickens's methods of characterization. How do
> those methods shape the novel's message?

In *A Tale of Two Cities,* Dickens repeatedly contrasts characters
in stark terms: if one seems virtuous, then the other will be cruel
and pitiable. Dickens then goes on to show that the virtuous and
cruel characters are not as different as they seem. Like these pairs of
characters, the cities of London and Paris prove to be surprisingly
similar in Dickens's novel. By establishing a pattern of false dichoto-
mies, or contrasting pairs, Dickens warns that London may have to
confront the same problems that tormented revolutionary France.

Readers often remember *A Tale of Two Cities* for its comic-book
juxtapositions of good and bad characters, upright citizens and
unrepentant sinners. Noble Darnay and vulgar Carton appear to
be inverse reflections of each other, their physical similarities under-
scoring their obvious spiritual differences. Darnay marries, starts a
family, and travels to France to help a friend; Carton drinks heavily and curses his wasted life. The two most prominent women in
the novel—Lucie and Madame Defarge—live by conflicting moral
codes. Golden-haired, pure-hearted Lucie exclaims that she has to
kneel to her "honoured father," whereas the dark, cold Madame
invests all her energy in cataloguing the men she wants to kill. Dickens also contrasts the Madame with the saintly Miss Pross, who
would never leave behind her motherly duties to begin a reign of
terror. These pairs of polar opposites appear throughout the novel.

Despite their unforgettable differences, Dickens's dichotomous
characters have many beliefs and attributes in common. For example, Carton and Darnay share a deep love for Lucie and a sense of
discomfort in regard to the past. (Carton regrets his drinking, and
Darnay regrets his family ties.) Madame Defarge's history—revealed
long after we meet her—includes a great deal of personal tragedy,
and Dickens makes clear that the Madame acts on the same feelings
of love and loyalty that motivate Lucie throughout the novel. Miss
Pross and Madame Defarge share a superhuman commitment to
their goals, to the extent that neither surrenders in a climactic gun-
fight over Lucie. Again and again, Dickens emphasizes the similarities between his saintly and villainous characters.

Like these falsely dichotomous characters, the cities of Paris and London share several unexpected problems, traditions, and open wounds. At first, the cities seem wildly different. Paris is witness to brutal class conflicts, whereas British citizens are not whispering about bloody revolution. The novel's opening scenes encourage us to see London as Paris's superior neighbor: Lucie, the beautiful Londoner, rescues her father from a dingy Parisian prison and declares that the best possible medicine is to "bring him home." Dickens associates London with the Darnays—a law-abiding, happily married couple with children—whereas he repeatedly links Paris to the Defarges—a nefarious husband and wife who distrust each other. But as the story unfolds, the differences between the cities begin to break down. London, Dickens reminds us, has recently had a wave of crime and capital punishment, and the anarchic British chimneysweep—accusing passersby of treason for "the pleasure of wreaking vengeance"—closely resembles the deranged Parisian peasants who trample one another to drink from a broken cask of wine. London is not the tranquil and emphatically un-Parisian capital that it once seemed to be.

By establishing a pattern of odd, unpredictable doubles, Dickens reinforces his idea that London may fall victim to the crises of the French Revolution. Dickens, the son of a poor man, resented the harsh treatment of Britain's impoverished citizens, and he used his novels to plead for economic justice. In *A Tale of Two Cities,* he shows that the world is full of misleading opposites: Heroes and villains alike must struggle with prejudices, doubts, and troubled pasts. The injustices that drove French peasants to wage war against the aristocracy could cause the same problems in England. Dickens leaves us with the haunting image of Lucie, knitting in her comfortable London home, but straining to hear distant, French footsteps in the streets.

GLOSSARY OF LITERARY TERMS

ANTAGONIST

The entity that acts to frustrate the goals of the *protagonist*. The antagonist is usually another *character* but may also be a non-human force.

ANTIHERO / ANTIHEROINE

A *protagonist* who is not admirable or who challenges notions of what should be considered admirable.

CHARACTER

A person, animal, or any other thing with a personality that appears in a *narrative*.

CLIMAX

The moment of greatest intensity in a text or the major turning point in the *plot*.

CONFLICT

The central struggle that moves the *plot* forward. The conflict can be the *protagonist*'s struggle against fate, nature, society, or another person.

FIRST-PERSON POINT OF VIEW

A literary style in which the *narrator* tells the story from his or her own *point of view* and refers to himself or herself as "I." The narrator may be an active participant in the story or just an observer.

HERO / HEROINE

The principal *character* in a literary work or *narrative*.

IMAGERY

Language that brings to mind sense-impressions, representing things that can be seen, smelled, heard, tasted, or touched.

MOTIF

A recurring idea, structure, contrast, or device that develops or informs the major *themes* of a work of literature.

NARRATIVE

A story.

NARRATOR

The person (sometimes a *character*) who tells a story; the *voice* assumed by the writer. The narrator and the author of the work of literature are not the same person.

PLOT

The arrangement of the events in a story, including the sequence in which they are told, the relative emphasis they are given, and the causal connections between events.

POINT OF VIEW

The *perspective* that a *narrative* takes toward the events it describes.

PROTAGONIST

The main *character* around whom the story revolves.

SETTING

The location of a *narrative* in time and space. Setting creates mood or atmosphere.

SUBPLOT

A secondary *plot* that is of less importance to the overall story but may serve as a point of contrast or comparison to the main plot.

SYMBOL

An object, *character,* figure, or color that is used to represent an abstract idea or concept. Unlike an *emblem,* a symbol may have different meanings in different contexts.

SYNTAX

The way the words in a piece of writing are put together to form lines, phrases, or clauses; the basic structure of a piece of writing.

THEME

A fundamental and universal idea explored in a literary work.

TONE

The author's attitude toward the subject or *characters* of a story or poem or toward the reader.

VOICE

An author's individual way of using language to reflect his or her own personality and attitudes. An author communicates voice through *tone, diction,* and *syntax.*

LITERARY ANALYSIS

A Note on Plagiarism

Plagiarism—presenting someone else's work as your own—rears its ugly head in many forms. Many students know that copying text without citing it is unacceptable. But some don't realize that even if you're not quoting directly, but instead are paraphrasing or summarizing, *it is plagiarism* unless you cite the source.

Here are the most common forms of plagiarism:

- Using an author's phrases, sentences, or paragraphs without citing the source
- Paraphrasing an author's ideas without citing the source
- Passing off another student's work as your own

How do you steer clear of plagiarism? You should *always* acknowledge all words and ideas that aren't your own by using quotation marks around verbatim text or citations like footnotes and endnotes to note another writer's ideas. For more information on how to give credit when credit is due, ask your teacher for guidance or visit www.sparknotes.com.

REVIEW & RESOURCES

QUIZ

1. *A Tale of Two Cities* opens in 1775. Which of the following does not characterize this period?

    A. The British colonies in America have just presented a list of grievances to the King of England.
    B. Crime plagues the streets of London.
    C. The guillotine stands as a much-feared fixture on the streets of Paris.
    D. The French aristocracy causes great suffering among the lower classes.

2. Why are the drivers of the Dover mail coach hesitant to stop for Jerry Cruncher's message?

    A. They fear that he is a highwayman attempting to rob the passengers.
    B. They fear that stopping will put them behind schedule for delivering the mail in a timely fashion.
    C. They have been charged with the safety of Jarvis Lorry, one of the coach's passengers.
    D. Jerry Cruncher's troublesome reputation precedes him.

3. What object does Doctor Manette keep during his imprisonment in order to escape "in spirit"?

    A. A picture of his wife and daughter
    B. The Bible
    C. A keg of wine
    D. A lock of his wife's hair

4. By what name do the men in Defarge's wine shop call their fellow revolutionaries?

    A. Jacques
    B. Pierre
    C. Jasper
    D. Xavier

5. What skill did Doctor Manette develop in order to pass the time during his incarceration?

    A.   Drawing
    B.   Whittling
    C.   Shoemaking
    D.   Storytelling

6. What symbol does Dickens use to portend the bloodshed of the French Revolution?

    A.   The Dover mail coach
    B.   The broken wine cask
    C.   Tellson's Bank
    D.   Madame Defarge's malevolent stare

7. During her testimony, to whom does Lucie claim that Charles Darnay alluded on the boat ride from Calais to Dover?

    A.   Louis XVI
    B.   John Adams
    C.   Napoleon Bonaparte
    D.   George Washington

8. After Darnay's acquittal, why does Sydney Carton claim to dislike him?

    A.   Darnay is unattractive and mean-spirited.
    B.   Darnay abuses the love of Lucie Manette.
    C.   Darnay reminds him of how far he has fallen and everything he might have been.
    D.   Even though he has been acquitted, Darnay is a traitor.

9. To which animal does Dickens compare Sydney Carton?

    A.   A jackal
    B.   A lion
    C.   A weasel
    D.   A sloth

10. *A Tale of Two Cities* was published in weekly installments from April to November of what year?

    A. 1845
    B. 1859
    C. 1879
    D. 1890

11. What image does Dickens frequently use to describe Lucie Manette?

    A. An earth-bound angel
    B. A golden thread
    C. A tiger lily
    D. A calm in a storm

12. What sound does Lucie often hear echoing off the street when she is in her home?

    A. Footsteps
    B. Brawling
    C. The yells of the crowd at public executions
    D. A choir singing

13. Which of the following characters is related to the Marquis, whose carriage runs down a small child?

    A. Doctor Manette
    B. Sydney Carton
    C. Charles Darnay
    D. Miss Pross

14. Who does Miss Pross believe is the ideal suitor for Lucie Manette?

    A. Sydney Carton
    B. Charles Darnay
    C. Her brother, Solomon
    D. She believes that no man is good enough for Lucie.

15. What does Mr. Lorry try to persuade Mr. Stryver not to do?

    A.   Propose to Lucie Manette
    B.   Invest his money in Tellson's Bank
    C.   Drop Sydney Carton as a business colleague
    D.   Visit Paris at a time of political turmoil

16. Who promises Lucie Manette that he would, if necessary, die for her?

    A.   Jarvis Lorry
    B.   Sydney Carton
    C.   Charles Darnay
    D.   Monsieur Defarge

17. What does Jerry Cruncher frequently go out to do at night?

    A.   Raid Tellson's Bank
    B.   Deliver messages to prisoners in the Bastille
    C.   Dig up bodies in the cemetery
    D.   Meet with other revolutionaries to plan uprisings

18. Who informs the Defarges that Lucie Manette has married Charles Darnay?

    A.   The mender of roads
    B.   Jarvis Lorry
    C.   Gaspard
    D.   John Barsad

19. On the night after Lucie and Charles are married, what does Doctor Manette do?

    A.   He prepares to join them on their honeymoon.
    B.   He reverts to his prison pastime of making shoes.
    C.   He confesses to Miss Pross that he thinks Lucie has made a terrible mistake.
    D.   He writes a letter to Defarge, asking him to spare Darnay's life.

20. During the storming of the Bastille, who decapitates the fortress's guard?

    A. Madame Defarge
    B. Defarge
    C. John Barsad
    D. An anonymous Jacques

21. Why does the Paris mob kill Foulon?

    A. Because he is a spy
    B. Because he suggested that starving people should eat grass
    C. Because his carriage ran down a child in the street
    D. Because he collected high taxes from the peasants

22. What is the duration of Manette's psychological relapse after Lucie leaves for her honeymoon?

    A. Nine days
    B. Four days
    C. A fortnight
    D. A year and three months

23. Who develops a habit of watching and speaking to Lucie as she waits on a Paris street corner each day, hoping that Darnay will be able to see her from his prison window?

    A. Madame Defarge
    B. Defarge
    C. A wood-sawyer
    D. A seamstress

24. Who does the spy John Barsad turn out to be?

    A. Miss Pross' brother, Solomon
    B. A relation of the Marquis Evrémonde
    C. Madame Defarge's long-lost brother
    D. Roger Cly

REVIEW & RESOURCES

25. Why was Doctor Manette imprisoned?

    A. He stole bread.
    B. He failed to save the life of an aristocrat's daughter.
    C. The Marquis Evrémonde feared that Manette would reveal one of the Marquis' dark secrets.
    D. He was an outspoken critic of the royal family.

ANSWER KEY

1: C; 2: A; 3: D; 4: A; 5: C; 6: B; 7: D; 8: C; 9: A; 10: B; 11: B; 12: A; 13: C; 14: C; 15: A; 16: B; 17: C; 18: D; 19: B; 20: A; 21: B; 22: A; 23: C; 24: A; 25: C

Suggestions for Further Reading

BECKWITH, CHARLES, ed. *Twentieth Century Interpretations of* A TALE OF TWO CITIES. Englewood Cliffs, NJ: Prentice-Hall, 1972.

BLOOM, HAROLD. *Charles Dickens's* A TALE OF TWO CITIES. New York: Chelsea House Publishers, 1987.

COTSELL, MICHAEL, ed. *Critical Essays on Charles Dickens's* A TALE OF TWO CITIES. New York: G. K. Hall, 1998.

GLANCY, RUTH. A TALE OF TWO CITIES: *An Annotated Bibliography.* New York: Garland, 1993.

———. A TALE OF TWO CITIES: *Dickens's Revolutionary Novel.* Boston: Twain Publishers, 1991.

NEWLIN, GEORGE. *Understanding* A TALE OF TWO CITIES: *A Student Casebook to Issues, Sources, and Historical Documents.* Westport, CT: Greenwood Press, 1998.

SANDERS, ANDREW. *The Companion to* A TALE OF TWO CITIES. London: Unwin Hyman, 1988.

SWISHER, CLARICE, ed. *Readings on Charles Dickens.* San Diego, CA: Greenhaven Press, 1998.